THINK FAST!!

Lessons I Learned From Minnesota to Manhattan and Back

Carole Peterson Wendt

Copyrighted © by Carole Wendt May 2025

For my brother Calvin Peterson,
And sister Myrna Joy Peterson Maher

PREFACE

This is a book of memories, daydreams, and speculations. No chapters, no list of contents, nothing in chronological order – a mixed bag like a box of candy or a tray of hors d'oeuvres.

Each piece stands alone – a fragment of my life as I went from a farm in Minnesota to Manhattan and back. I laughed with Sophia Loren, took communion from Pope John Paul, chatted with Paul Newman, and worked with Jack Paar, David Frost, Tom Brokaw, Barbara Walters, and David Brinkley.

Because the content is presented in bits and pieces, it is the kind of book that can be picked up and read when there are only a few moments to kill – like standing in line, waiting for a stoplight, or sitting in a doctor's waiting room.

I used to read walking down the street in Manhattan. Concerned passers-by warned me I might fall in a hole or get run over by a car. Never did.

Now, please read on and enjoy stories from the life I loved – but maybe better not read in the street.

THINK FAST!!

The "think fast" lesson began on a Minnesota farm where I lived until I was eight years old. Our nearest neighbor was a mile away. Playmates other than my siblings were hard to come by. I tried playing with the neighbor boy. But that went badly. We were sitting in the chicken coop eating chicken feed – it's not bad tasting, by the way. Everything was going well until he did something I didn't like. I threw a stick at him and hit him in the head. Blood trickled down his forehead as he screamed for his mother. I, of course, immediately left the scene of the crime and ran lickety-split back home. I raced upstairs and pretended to read the newspaper.

It didn't take long before my mother called out, "Carole, come on down here."

The jig was up. I was told never, ever throw things at anyone unless it was part of a game and the receiver was ready for it.

That made sense and my brother heeded that rule. In his own way. He'd shout,

"Think fast!" and within a heartbeat, he'd hurl something at me and I was supposed to snatch it out of the air with lightning reflexes. I got good at that. And it stood me in good stead decades later in the middle of a Manhattan restaurant.

It went like this:

I was then producing and writing for the David Frost show. After we taped the show, we would often go next door to Sardi's for dinner.

This evening I was sitting with the producer, Bob Carman, at the very back of the place. David Frost came in and sat down right beside the entrance a long way across the restaurant from me. David was an athlete as a young man, playing rugby in college and was still in good shape. The restaurant was crowded and everyone looked up when he shouted across the large room, "Carole!"

With that he lofted a small football-shaped hard roll at me high above the crowd. Shades of "Think fast!" came back to me as it sailed high above me. Without hesitation and almost without looking, I reached up, snatched it right out of the air, turned to Bob and without a pause continued our conversation.

David's mouth fell open and the diners broke into applause. I shook the roll at David and took a nice big bite out of it, happy to know I could still "think fast."

OLDTIMER OUTFITS

When I do chores around my house, I wear what I call oldtimer outfits – the kind of clothes you wouldn't be caught dead in if you had any pride. But I'm a very senior citizen and I don't care what I look like when I'm mucking about in the yard.

My favorite ensemble includes a pair of ancient pants that look awful. They are light blue cotton and too big. The elastic waist band has stretched over time and now that I've lost some weight, they keep sliding off me. I have to stop every so often and hitch them back up. Because they hang so low, they've gotten muddy and nothing I can do will get rid of the dark stains on the bottom of the legs. Plus, one leg has white spots where I accidentally sprinkled some Clorox on it. My solution is to roll up both legs to just below the knee. Add a paint-spattered oversize blue man's shirt and you have my working wardrobe. Stunning.

You might ask: "Why not buy a new pair of pants?" Because I HATE TO SHOP.

"Okay," you might say," why not take a few stitches in the waistband so the pants don't fall off?"

To that, I say, "My arthritic fingers hurt when I thread a needle and try to sew." (Alright, maybe I'll try a safety pin, happy now?)

My mother would be horrified by my appearance.

"Why do you always wear jeans?" she said when I visited one summer. "You're from New York City, you should dress better than that."

I said, "This is me. I wear jeans to work. All my co-workers dress casually; we aren't bankers after all. Informal dress is a symbol of our elite status; we are creative artists." (You may question whether journalists are "elite" or even "creative" but I was laying it on thick to make a point.)

So, there I am in my oldtimer outfit wrestling my garden hose and careening about the yard trying to water my thirsty flowers, bushes, and trees. That hose is ancient and very stiff. You might suggest, "Why not buy a new hose that's more flexible?" Remember? I hate to shop. Plus, I don't want to go to stores anyway, unless I absolutely must, as when I am running out of food or gas.

I remember once at the Today Show, I had come to the office on a Saturday to do some last minute work. I thought the place was empty when I heard some heavy shuffling footsteps in the hall. I looked up and there galumphing past my office door was Tom Brokaw. He had on an oldtimer outfit. Cap pulled down over his ears (it was winter) a huge beatup oversize jacket, and some old baggy pants shoved into galoshes.

We both laughed and I said, "Well, there goes the hick from Yankton."

He teased me back, "You're a bigger hick than I am. At least Yankton has a K-mart."

That was a few years ago, needless to say. Today, both Yankton and Litchfield have Walmarts, so I guess Tom and I are even now.

DON'T DRIVE WHILE WASHING YOUR CLOTHES

I think we can all agree that it's a no-no to drive while using a cell phone or putting on makeup. But people do. And should not.

Here's what I did wrong while driving. I was racing to Burnsville for my brother's 90th birthday party. With road construction on the way and more traffic as a result it was taking longer than usual. I was afraid I'd be late. I did not speed but I was tense. I took a sip of coffee, and dang, I spilled some of it on my white blouse.

Now, we all know you have to douse coffee stains with water right away or you'll never get them out. I did not want to show up looking like a pinto pony…my white blouse with beige spots all over it. Now, here I did the wrong thing: I decided to spot clean my blouse while driving.

I grabbed a paper towel and doused it with water from a cup in the cup holder next to the coffee. Keeping a sharp eye on the road, I smashed the soaking paper towel onto the spots on my blouse.

And lo! They came right out but of course I was soaked to the skin. But, I knew the blouse would dry in time since I had another 45 minutes before I got to the party.

Driving while doing my laundry reminded me of my nephew's confession to me that years ago he had the habit of reading books while zooming down the freeway. He quit doing that when he became a father. He realized he had a responsibility to stay alive for them and finally faced the fact that he was a serious menace on the road.

I used to read while walking. I did that often but finally quit at the urging of those who feared I'd hurt myself. However, I was often careless about untied shoelaces. I did not bother to tie them when they came loose. If I were in a hurry, I'd just ignore them and race on. Concerned New Yorkers passing by could not resist trying to help.

"Your shoelace is untied."

"I know," I'd say, as I swept along.

It seemed a waste of time to stop and tie my laces; I could do that when I got to where I was hurrying. I did find it rather charming that so-called cold New Yorkers were so concerned about my welfare. At least, when it came to laces.

It was an untied lace that resulted in a sweet situation.

I was in Hollywood with the Today Show. My assignment was to pre-interview Lucille Ball; she was in her dressing room on the movie set for *Mame* in which she was starring.

We sat across from each other in her dressing room chatting pleasantly, when she suddenly jumped up and lunged toward me. I thought, "What did I do? Is she angry?" Not at all.

She dropped to her knees in front of me and said, "Your shoelace is untied. You shouldn't run around like that. You could trip and hurt yourself."

With that she tied that shoelace firmly. Then, she jumped up and sat back down.

I thought, now there is a woman of action. She sees a problem and solves it just like that. No wonder she was one of the most successful actresses and producers in the business. A lesson learned. And all because I was lazy about tying my shoelaces.

By the way, in my senior years, I don't wear shoes with laces. Too hard on my back leaning over to tie them.

DRAGGED INTO THE MODERN WORLD

As I watched "Downton Abbey" for the third time, I heard the younger characters saying to the older ones -- when they object to electricity, or some other newfangled invention -- "You have got to join the modern age."

That's how I feel about computers, cell phones, tablets, laptops –well, you get the idea. I am also slowly being dragged into the modern world. I do use a computer and cell phone not connected to the internet. But then I added a new techie toy: ZOOM.

Okay, it's been around forever and millions use it but I have only lately joined the crowd. One friend takes college courses through Zoom, others check in with grandchildren. I had watched interviews conducted via Zoom so I was a bit up to speed on its uses.

The other day I got the idea to set up a Zoom meeting of the Litchfield Writers Group –a bunch of us who get together every month to improve our writing. Of course, we had not been able to do that during Covid. To get that Zoom meeting going, I had to make some changes:

First, I needed a camera. My computer did not have one. So, I bought a webcam and it now sits on top of the screen. I was good to go.

But first, as a kind of rehearsal, I asked Mike McNeil, who is in the group, and knows this stuff, to set up a chat for us. He did.

What fun. We laughed a lot, deciding which angle of our faces looked better and what we could set up as a background. We figured a bookcase in Mike's office would be appropriate for him and I put a sculpture of a bird on my kitchen table as a setting for my "scene."

As I saw myself on screen, I realized right away -- I definitely needed someone to do lighting, makeup and hair for my Zoom appearance. How did I look?

As Charlie Brown would say, "AAUUGHH!"

I remember once I was working with a former Miss America on a story for the Today Show. Snapshots were taken and later, she and I looked at them. I moaned about how awful I looked.

She kindly said "Carole, it's all in the lighting."

Come on, YOU pose next to a Miss America, it is NOT all in the lighting. But, she was partly right. The lighting in my kitchen is NOT set up to flatter me on Zoom. And hair and makeup? Help.

Now, put away vanity. I told myself. It'll be fun and it will really be a pleasure to see my computer screen filled with ten faces as we virtually reunite for the first time since the horrid plague began.

I was brave and zoomed away. It was well worth it.

ON THE LINE AT THE FACTORY

I worked at the Litchfield Produce Company in the mid-1950's to earn money for college. I chose that company, formed in March of 1912, because it offered the best pay I could get in Litchfield. As the only union shop in the city, the Company's hourly wage was higher than most.

I didn't know much about what occurred inside those factory walls. My mother had worked there for years and when I visited her on the job, I was put off by the smell of ammonia, among other odors.

No smell put me off though when I needed money to go to the University of Minnesota. I applied, got hired, and at sixteen became a member of the Produce work force and its union, the Amalgamated Meatcutters and Butcher Workmen's Association, affiliated with the AFL/CIO.

I also began my education in what it takes to turn poultry into food. Like this:

The birds came from the noisy chicken farms of Melrose, from the dusty turkey ranches of

Litchfield and from many other poultry-growing areas of the nation.

After a bumpy trip in the back of an open truck, the fowl arrived at the plant and were tossed into the galley, a warehouse full of tall racks divided into cages housing four turkeys or six chickens.

They were kept and fed in the cages until they were needed, usually about a week. The last day they were not fed. This emptied their crops and that made cleaning them simpler.

When an order came in, the cages were emptied of the number of turkeys or chickens called for. The racks were rolled up to a moving overhead chain. The wildly flapping birds were attached to it by their legs; at this point they didn't have long to live.

Death was quick: they were zapped by an electric knife which electrocuted them and slit their throats to drain their blood. The bleeding insured cleanliness and the whiteness of the meat.

After the killing, the birds moved into a tank of boiling water where they remained for about fifteen seconds; this loosened their feathers. As they slid out of the tank, their bodies passed by the winger, a machine resembling a washing machine roller. A worker placed each bird's wings into the roller which pulled off the long feathers. Next, the bird moved through the buffers. Like a car wash, this machine had long snakelike straps attached to revolving cylinders moving in opposite directions. As the bird moved through it, the straps slapped most of the feathers off its sides and legs.

Operators had to be careful so the machine didn't bruise the birds' flesh. Spring chickens were most easily bruised while turkeys could withstand the full force of the buffers without turning blue.

After the buffers were through with them; they next went to the pickers, workers who removed what feathers were left and examined them for cleanliness. If the floor lady decided any were not clean enough, they were put through again.

Next, the birds descended into the basement where workers cut off their legs –below the drumstick –with a paper cutter type tool.

Up again from the basement they went to the eviscerating part of the plant. This department was kept cool and clean. Here, the defeathered animal became oven-ready.

Each bird was inspected for cleanliness and "pinned" which meant all the feather roots left behind were removed by hand by workers called "pinners."

Next, the birds moved through a washer which directed blasts of water all over and inside them. Then, their crops were removed, the contents dropped into a trough where running water swooshed it away to a tank.

Before the bird was disemboweled, it was cut deftly and cleanly inside the left leg –a cut no more than three inches on a chicken or five inches on a turkey. This opening allowed the eviscerators, or, as they were called in the plant, the "drawers," to reach into the bird, remove all the entrails, and place them on a conveyor belt. A licensed veterinarian inspected the heart, lungs, liver, and intestines of each bird. If he found any evidence of disease or decay in the entrails, he tossed the bird into the garbage.

He could also stop the chain any time he saw fit. Paid by the Federal government, he owed no allegiance to the company; his job was to safeguard the public.

After the birds passed inspection, the hearts, livers, and gizzards were separated from the entrails and cleaned. The insides of the birds were further cleaned and scraped with saw-tooth scrapers. The tiny inedible oil gland at the base of the tail was cut out. The head was clipped off at the last vertebra to save as much of the neck as possible. Finally, the bird moved into the last washer, and continued on to the packaging plant.

The birds were put into tanks, covered with chipped ice, and allowed to cool for a minimum of four hours. When needed, they were brought out and placed on another chain and sent to the packing department.

Once again, they were inspected for cleanliness and for grading. If they were bruised or slightly deformed, they were labeled a "B." If they were cut on the breastbone, or greatly deformed, or very thin, they were labelled "C"s. An "A" bird had no flaws. If a bird needed more cleaning, this department took care of it.

After being graded and cleaned, they moved on to "baggers" who inserted bags containing a heart, liver, and gizzard into each bird. For hens, a piece of fat was also included. Each bird was then fitted into a bag of its own.

If the Produce was preparing birds for another meat packer, that company's brand would be imprinted on the bag. It could be a different company every week.

Turkeys were tied around the legs and tail to make them fit better into their bags. A pneumatic machine sucked the air out of the bag and a sealer clipped the open end shut.

The packaged birds then tumbled into a large, oven like machine called a steamer which sealed the package around the entire body of the bird. They rolled through this machine and came tumbling out onto a table. Here, a worker placed each on a scale and marked its weight and grade on the package. The birds were sorted according to grade and put in bins. From there they were placed in boxes, cardboard or wooden, according to the order. Six large hens or four turkeys would fill a box. The boxes were then stacked in another cooler, awaiting shipment.

This process could turn out oven-ready birds quickly; about 28 chickens or ten turkeys a minute.

During my several summers of work at the factory, I was assigned just about every job in the process. I cut the heads off the dead birds as they came by on the chain; I pulled the guts out of them; I removed the feathers; and I packaged them when they were ready for shipping.

I also processed eggs at the Produce. As a "candler," I held eggs in front of a light to see if they were good or not. Good eggs were transparent enough so that the yolk could be seen floating about inside. Bad eggs were dark. That either meant they were rotten or they were fertilized and had an embryonic chick inside. Unusable either way.

As a "breaker," I stood in a well-lit room, in contrast to the candling room which had to be dark. Here we cracked open the eggs; sniffed the shells; and dumped the yolk and white into a pail. If the egg smelled bad, we threw it into a huge barrel along with the discarded shells.

When our pails of good eggs were full, we brought them up to a metal table to be dumped into large barrels. The eggs were then dried and shipped out to customers; often they went to the United States Army.

The egg breaking room was large and high ceilinged. Sound echoed loudly in it. As many as thirty people worked in the room, all of them women. Almost all the line workers at the Produce were women. Almost all the managers and foremen were men.

It was hard, tiring work. But there was fun, too. I remember one game we used to play in the egg breaking room. Every four workers shared a large barrel for the broken eggs shells. These had to be crushed down from time to time to make room for more shells. To do that, we used a large heavy metal "stomper" with a long handle on it which stood in the middle of the barrel.

The stomping made a quite satisfying, deep, resounding thump. Every so often, and frequently instigated by my mischievous mother, a stomping session would start. Two resounding thumps would suddenly reverberate around the room; then another; then another, until everyone was pounding away like a runaway drum line.

Then, almost on cue, the foreman would come running into the room shouting, "Ladies, ladies, now stop that, and get back to work."

And then, all those usually well behaved ladies from the farms and homes in and around Litchfield would laugh and tease him, stop their play; and get back to the business of factory work.

Strong, lifelong friendships came out of those workrooms. And tragedy. A fire raced through the building once badly burning several workers. Another time, when I was working there, an ammonia pipe burst. The strong, choking gas swiftly spread through the building. I ran out in a panic. As I raced away, I saw my mother stay behind helping others out a window before she escaped herself.

Later, I was secretly ashamed of myself for escaping alone, but I was very proud of my mother for her bravery.

That job helped pay for my college education. It also taught me how to stick to a difficult job and to respect and get along with my fellow workers.

Once, when I was a secretary in an office, and a co-worker complained about her job, I remembered those days "on the line" at the Produce.

I said, "You know, when I worked in the factory, standing all day long, we would talk about how great it would be to have a 'sit-down' job. Well, here we are, we've got 'sit-down' jobs. It can't be all that bad, now, can it?"

TALKING TO STRANGERS

Once upon a time, I interviewed people for a living. I did so many interviews that after awhile I started talking to people – even when it wasn't for a job -- as if I were interviewing them.

I was criticized for this sometimes because onlookers thought my subjects would take offense at my nosiness. I found that no one took offense; actually they were pleased.

Who wouldn't be when you think about it? If you met someone who seemed fascinated by you and wanted to know all about you, wouldn't you love it? If you were in the Witness Protection Program or a criminal on the lam, you probably would not like it, but most folks really warmed to my interrogations. I was genuinely interested.

But the bad part was that once I had their story, at least as much as I wanted to know, I backed off on the conversation. That puzzled some people who thought they had found a new best friend. Sometimes, we did become friends but often not. I would take my leave but I could tell they were confused by the intense interest that had faded quickly.

When I realized I was being hurtful at times, I tried to shut off my professional technique in social situations. I still do it though when I cannot resist finding out about an interesting person doing an interesting thing.

I am always surprised how much a stranger will tell a curious stranger. I don't have to worry about telling my story since they usually are so fascinated talking about themselves they almost never think to ask me anything. Which is fine with me; I am not there to tell my story but to get theirs.

I have on occasion embarrassed my friends and family by being so inquisitive. Once, my husband and I were chugging through New York City Bay on a ferry boat. Bill and I were standing on a balcony overlooking the captain at work.

I said to Bill, "I wonder if he ever comes across a corpse floating in the Bay."

All Bill said was "Oh, no, you don't."

My brother likes to interview people too; it runs in the family, I think. We were at the museum in Alexandria where the celebrated Kensington Runestone is kept. We both noticed a guard standing nearby.

I said, "I'm going to ask him some questions."

My brother said, "No you're not. I'm going to talk to him; you talked to the last guard."

We had to divvy up our subjects. Leave my brother alone in any public place for two minutes and you will return to find him deep in conversation with someone, anyone, nearby. I asked him if he noticed that people were puzzled when he'd gotten the story and moved on.

"Yes," he said, "they get confused and wonder why I'm so interested and then just say good bye and walk away."

Years ago, as a child, I was painfully shy. Being fair skinned, I'd blush very obviously when anyone paid attention to me. I think by developing such an intense interest in other people I overcame that early timidity. I got my attention off myself and onto others.

People are fascinating. I like to try to figure out what makes them tick; why do they do what they do? Others have said to me that I get too involved in trying to figure people out.

One friend said, "Who cares why they do what they do? They do it and that's the end of it. Forget it."

I say, "But why? What brought them to it?"

I guess I'm not alone in this curiosity; if I were, there would be no books, plays, or in fact anything written anywhere. It all begins with curiosity, doesn't it?

ADVANTAGE OF DIRTY WINDOWS

I like looking out of clear and clean windows. But not enough to wash them. But wait, before you condemn me for being a lazy housekeeper – which I am, by the way, but wait, hear me out.

My house is very old, built around 1880, originally a log cabin, so the window frames are, shall we say? A bit dated. And warped. So I can not get them open enough to remove them to clean both sides of the indoor and outdoor windows.

I was so frustrated I decided to have brand new windows put in. When I described my plan to my nephew Chuck (who runs his own construction company and knows about stuff like that), he was aghast. And when Chuck is aghast, he's really aghast.

"What are you saying? You want to spend over $20,000 to have clean window panes?"

I saw his point right away. $20,000 Wow. That's about 7 trips to Europe. I decided I can see through those windows well enough after all. Chuck suggested I hire a professional window washer. I thought about that but forgot all about it. I was too busy planning my seven trips to Europe.

So that was one advantage of having dirty windows, but just the other day I realized there is another advantage – one that's much more important than any European safari. Dirty windows prevent bird suicides.

That's right. My cousin Natalie in Iowa told me the other day that two cardinals killed themselves fighting their own images in her spanking clean window panes. Plus a robin has been butting his head against her living room window for days. She figures his head must be harder than the cardinals' heads. Still, that might not end well.

But see? That's the big advantage of my dirty windows. No bird has ever fought his image in my panes. He can't see himself for the dirt.

I rest my case.

GOODBYE TO ALL THAT

On May 16, 2015, I locked the door to my apartment in Manhattan and left for good. I had lived there since 1960 with my husband Bill. He died in 1998 of cancer.

We both thought I would move back to our home state of Minnesota almost immediately after his death. But I didn't. I stuck around for another 17 years, but, as time passed, I came to realize the city no longer suited me.

Every year, for six months, after Bill died, I lived in Litchfield. We had bought my parents' home after my widowed mother moved into a nursing home. It had also been my grandparents' home and it felt right for me to own that house.

Bill agreed but only because it mattered so much to me. It turned out to be a very good decision because when we knew he would die of cancer we were glad I would have a home near family and friends.

I knew it was right to leave New York City but I wondered just how it would feel to walk out that door for the last time, and found that moving was backbreaking.

For 55 years I had never had to figure out what to do with all my belongings. What to discard and what to give away and what to keep. Big questions. I made so many lists I almost needed a list of my lists.

Charities turned me down because I was not willing to email photos of my furniture. Plus that, they would not pick up. I did finally find a charity that would take some of my things. My landlady said she was going to renovate my place so I could leave whatever I couldn't get rid of. That took care of that problem.

I had to throw out huge bagsful of dishes, pots, pans, silverware, bedding, old suitcases, and other odds and ends. A neighbor was glad to take my TV set, paper towels, napkins, and cleaning supplies.

That worked out well; in gratitude, he was eager to help me haul out several heavy bags of other items we didn't want.

The night before I was to fly out and leave for good I walked through the half-empty rooms --- remembering my life at 79 Thompson Street, New York City.

I felt sad. The rooms still looked occupied. No one would take the bed, sofa, bookcases, Persian rug, or kitchen table and chairs.

The landlady had come by the day before to say goodbye and reassure me that she would get rid of whatever I had to leave. I looked at the kitchen. The floor had a patch I had glued into the linoleum. A tile had worn through and I had repaired it myself. It was a pattern I could not find in New York City but I got lucky on a car trip through Minnesota. I discovered that the motel owner where I stopped for an overnight had redone the floors in his rooms; the linoleum was the pattern I was looking for. I guessed he might have some left over and sure enough he did.

So for five dollars I bought a remnant, carted it to New York and found it matched my kitchen floor. Of course, it was new so it was quite obvious when set into the old linoleum. But, it was the same pattern and I hadn't had to redo the whole floor.

The big kitchen window had a folding metal grate over it. We had to put it there after we were robbed. The thieves – probably teenagers -- took $400 cash but left behind an empty can of Coca Cola and a half eaten ham sandwich. They had entered by pushing in the door.

We had to have it replaced because it no longer closed properly. That was the only time we were ever robbed in all the years we lived in New York City. Police guessed it might have been a crime of opportunity; there was a vocational school for problem students nearby and the cops said they sometimes caused problems. They were never caught.

The neighborhood was known to be quite safe; crime was rare in our area. I remembered how it was when we first moved in. We were the only tenants who were not Italian. There were men's clubs in each block; the members would sit and play cards and keep an eye on the streets. It did not go well with you if they caught you doing something they did not like. I would often find guys in the entry to our building playing the numbers – an illegal gambling game popular in the neighborhood.

We took over the apartment from friends, Diane and Bette, who were moving to Spain. Diane was a co-worker of mine at American Airlines, and my first friend in New York.

She told us, "If anyone bothers you on the street, just yell 'Tony' and half the neighborhood will come running."

She wasn't exaggerating. Once a candy store owner refused to pay me $40 I had won on a scratch-off card; he was an Indian immigrant and his English failed him.

I stepped into the street and said to a group of men standing outside, "Hey, this guy won't pay me my forty bucks."

I showed them my card. In the store one guy said, "Give the lady her money, fella."

He got the message and paid up immediately. You didn't fool with the guys in the neighborhood.

Our building was built in 1800, designed to house immigrants, most of them Italian. Cold water flats they were called; with no hot water and no bathtubs. The families used to go to public baths nearby. Later, bathtubs were added. When we first moved in, our bathtub was in the kitchen with a large board covering it. It also served as a counter.

After a few years, the landlord rearranged the kitchen so that the bathtub could be enclosed in a separate small room. The toilet remained in its own tiny room. The kitchen was smaller as a result but we could at least bathe in privacy.

We had moved to the neighborhood from the upper West Side of Manhattan where the population was predominantly immigrant Puerto Ricans. Teenage boys would make kissing sounds or whistle at me as I passed by; it was quite different on Thompson Street. Italian boys made no such sounds; in fact, did not acknowledge that I was present.

They were taught to respect girls and women walking by. If they misbehaved, the grandmas leaning out the windows would give them a good talking to. It was just not done. Once you were seen to be a resident, you were protected.

Once I heard a grandma shouting to a teenage boy leaning on a car. "Get off that car, kid. That doesn't belong to you."

He leaped away from it as if he'd been burned. Sometimes, those grandmas would yell down to a child or grandchild on the street, telling them to go to the store. They'd lower a basket on a rope with money in it and off the kid would go to the deli.

He'd come back and yell, "Hey, Grandma, lower the basket."

She would; he'd put in the bread and milk and pasta, and up it'd go. No stair climbing necessary – there were no elevators in those tenements.

Our building had no elevator either. The floors were numbered in the European way: The first floor was the main floor; and what we'd call the second floor was called the first floor and so on. I always told people we lived on the second floor as that's what it said on the wall outside our door. It was actually the third floor.

Bill was a professional singer and to exercise his voice he studied opera and often practiced by singing arias in the apartment. One summer day he was singing "Nemico della Patria" from the opera Andrea Chenier – a beautiful dramatic song. His big baritone voice floated out through our third floor window that opened onto the street.

He was amazed when he finished; applause broke out on the sidewalk below. Several people had gathered to listen to him. He leaned out the window and took a bow to more applause.

The neighborhood, being Italian, was mostly Catholic so the local church, Saint Anthony of Padua, was influential in community activities. There was the annual festival. It took up two whole blocks and was filled with Italian food vendors. Zeppoles were luscious -- hunks of dough mixed in big cauldrons, then thrown into hot fat to rise and turn brown. They were fished out, sprinkled with sugar and sold by the dozens. Pizza stands lined the street and fresh clams and oysters were also sold -- opened for you on the spot. Bowls of pasta were also on offer covered with delicious sauces – such as marinara, shrimp Alfredo, and white or red clam sauce. Lights were strung across the street from building to building and people came from all over the city. Years later, the festival was deemed too noisy and maybe not profitable enough so it was canceled.

I remember once years ago watching hundreds of people marching silently in the street below our window. The local parishioners were honoring the Virgin Mary.

The procession was headed by a large statue of Mary carried by a dozen young men. The priest followed the statue and the congregation came behind him. That too finally ended. The neighborhood changed and was not predominantly Italian anymore.

The upscale crowd came in to renovate the coveted Greenwich Village apartments and the area was renamed Soho, meaning South of Houston. Houston is a street running east and west forming a northern border to this totally made up geographical distinction. Starting in the 80's, Soho became a quite desirable place to live. It became chic, the place to go.

For example, one day several years ago, I saw Gwyneth Paltrow and Brad Pitt buying pizza at my favorite parlor across the street from my building. Another time, as I waited to buy a sandwich at my deli, I realized the tall, dark gaunt man in front of me was the Academy Award winning actor Daniel Day Lewis. Sandra Bullock bought a house a block from my street. Prices everywhere went up and up.

A small restaurant and pastry shop in my block, Dominique Ansel, was featured in the New Yorker as the place to go. Soon, long lines started in front of it at 6 AM. They were there to buy the now famed "cronut" created by chef Dominique.

The Internet spread the news. And the crowds came. The "cronut" was a combination croissant and doughnut. I was able to get one and it was delicious. My niece, Eunice, visited me and decided she would get up at 5am, stand in line and get us a couple samples of this fashionable treat. The irony was that she did not like it after all; too sweet, she said. I loved it but never got another; I am not standing in line at 6 AM. No way. I do have some standards.

The change in the neighborhood helped our social life. When we first moved into our apartment, it was difficult getting people to visit us. The area was not attractive. It was clean and safe but not glamorous at all.

My mother came to see us and when she arrived, she gently asked me, "Is this a slum?" Her standards were Minnesotan. Litchfield had no dirty streets, no bums sleeping in doorways, no suspicious characters asking for small change.

I said, "No, Mother, the people who live here are all hardworking Italians; good Catholics all and there is no crime here; the guys see to that."

She was satisfied her daughter was safe. Before Soho became a swank area, it was bordered by a factory and warehouse district which was busy during the day; but at night everyone went home and there was no one around. A bit spooky. But, once the change set in and it became fancier with factory spaces turned into lofts by new arrivals, many of them rich and famous, we had no trouble getting people to come over.

It was much more interesting and safe. Fine restaurants opened their doors; high end boutiques popped up on West Broadway, one block over from Thompson. The local pizza parlor bragged that Madonna was a customer and had a newspaper clipping to prove it.

Movie directors set up location shoots in front of our building. Almost every day one street or another was shut off and we'd see stars like Jude

Law, Nick Nolte, and Willem DaFoe waiting for a call to act. I would go to movies set in New York City and see my favorite movie theater, my laundry, or Milady, the local bar, used as background for LAW AND ORDER or some other movie or TV show.

Location scouts loved our area. It had character and could be also used for period pieces. Saint Anthony of Padua Catholic Church, a block from our house, was used for exterior shots for the wedding in THE GODFATHER. I remember sitting in the Bleecker Street Cinema watching a Woody Allen movie in which the main character is seen sitting in the Bleecker Street Cinema. I had to laugh; I live in a movie set.

It was dead quiet at times, unexpected in such a busy and heavily populated area. But it could be insanely noisy. For years, the locals would stage a deafening July 4th fireworks celebration.

They would pile up a huge hill of explosives at the intersection half a block from our street-side windows. Then, they'd light it and – I timed it once – for 45 minutes the roar of exploding firecrackers thundered through the streets. I called the cops thinking they would care. "Oh, yeah, lady, they do that." End of conversation.

One year I was told some windows had broken from the sound waves. Next day the papers left from the explosives were a foot deep on the street. That was another tradition that, happily, finally ended.

Fire trucks whooped their way down our street frequently. I came to ignore the sound as do most New Yorkers. If it isn't my building, forget it. But during her visit my mother heard the trucks and always wondered what was happening. I'd reassure her that the trucks came by a lot and not to pay any attention to them.

But one night she said, "Carole, there's a fire."

I said, "Sure, Mother, don't worry. We hear sirens a lot here."

"No," she said, "there really is a fire."

I said, patiently, "Not to worry, Mother. It'll be okay."

She said, more urgently, "But wait. I see smoke next door."

I leapt out of bed to look myself; sure enough, there was a fire next door. I had to eat my words.

It turned out we were safe and the fire was soon taken care of. Our local firemen put it out fast. Sadly, some of those firemen lost their lives years later in the World Trade Center disaster.

There were tragedies in our building. One woman leaped to her death from the roof, egged on by her abusive husband who stood on the street below, yelling, "Jump!" He moved out and his sweet little daughter grew up to become a production assistant at a TV studio.

Tragically, she too elected to take her mother's way out, leaping to her death from the roof of a building up the street. Another tenant, a former postal worker, blew part of his right hand off playing with a firecracker. Crazy Curtis, he was known as. Harmless to others but not to himself. He moved out, too, after a while.

On the happier side, there was Jeff, who practiced the violin from time to time. Nice sound wafting through the hall.

Rocky, an immigrant from Italy and a longtime resident, told me, after Bill died, that he would be happy to lend me a hand if I needed anything. It was reassuring to have him across the hall.

I was part of the apartment house family. A family that gradually changed from all Italian to upwardly mobile young people who dressed perfectly, mostly in black, the New York City most favored color, and raced up and down the stairs with high energy. They were always friendly and sweet. The rents were extremely high so those young folks soon realized living in Soho may be fashionable but ultimately too expensive. The turnover in tenants speeded up. An average rent might be around $1500 to $2500 depending on the size of the apartment.

Some of us still had rent controlled or stabilized apartments so our rents remained in a more reasonable range. Apartments rented at market price, or whatever the landlord could get, and rose to high levels.

Where the names on the mailboxes once were all Italian but ours; now, there was only one Italian name listed – Rocky, my neighbor across the hall.

The tenants weren't all benign. The landlady told me she had had to evict a prostitute ring from the floor below me. A tenant across the hall from the brothel had complained about comings and goings that seemed very suspicious. They were and out went the prostitutes. I never noticed a thing.

Except for the occasional noisy neighbor playing music too loud late at night or too early in the morning, I didn't have much trouble with tenants.

On my sentimental journey through my apartment, the day before I left, I took a look around my living room. It still held my sofa, bookcase, mirror, light fixtures and our royal blue Persian rug. I had to leave it all. I was just was not up to carting any of it to Minnesota.

The Persian rug was a treasure. We bought it at a sale. The salesman said it was worth $7,000 but would sell it for $700. We bought that story and the rug, about 30 years ago. Lili chewed on it once and threw up. It was witness to dozens of parties, poetry and play readings, and Bill's acting lessons. He coached actors in our home from time to time.

House guests slept on the sofa that pulled out into a bed. Brother in law Wayne was shocked out of a dead sleep when our cat jumped on him. We had played with her by lying on the sofa and scratching our fingers on the upholstery to make her leap up. She chose to race into the room and bounce off the sofa and race away.

Wayne was not amused by the cat attack. In fact, now that I think more about it, Marvin, another brother in law, was also attacked in the middle of the night and so was a girl friend of mine who stayed overnight one time. They were not hurt but seriously shocked.

That cat. She lived 21 years. Always indoors with a few dramatic excursions outdoors. With Bill often working away from home, Lili and I became very good friends. We'd even watch television together.

She preferred nature shows on PBS; like me, she hated commercials. We both liked shows about cats and monkeys and birds. At night if there was a noise, she'd look at me and I'd say "Not to worry; it's nothing."

She'd turn away and go back to sleep. But, if it was a suspicious sound, I'd say, "We'd better check this out."

We'd both get up and investigate. It was always nothing and we'd go back to bed. But one time, it was something. She and I were sitting on the sofa one day when we heard alarming sounds on the street, not the usual noise. She and I raced to the window. A woman had been hit by a bus. There was blood on the street, lots of screaming, and what looked like pieces of flesh torn from her leg.

Lili was a calico cat. Once I called the vet because she seemed sick. I told him she was a calico cat.

He said, "A female, I assume."

I said, "How can you tell that over the phone?"

"Almost all calicos are female; if they're male, they can be worth ten thousand dollars," he said.

She recovered from whatever she had – probably too much rug eating. She died at 21 several years ago and my heart still hurts when I think of her.

We had many visitors who came to New York on business and stopped by for some fun. We were both in show business and led a somewhat unconventional life. Dick, Bill's sister's husband, ordinarily a serious engineer for Minnesota Mining, came to town from time to time. He thought of New York City as a lively place. Once, we were in the middle of a party, when he arrived at our apartment cheerfully waving a bottle of Scotch and happily shouting, "Party time!!" And it was. For many years.

My sister Myrna and Marvin, her husband, stayed with us for two weeks. Because I worked in TV, I could occasionally get free press seats to various shows.

To surprise them, we got tickets to a show in which the actors appeared nude in a scene or two. Those were the days when it was popular to include nudity in even the most serious play or musical. We did not prepare them for what was to come. They were shocked and then laughed a lot.

"Never saw a show like that," Myrna said.

We programmed their two weeks chock full of sightseeing. So much so that I think we exhausted them.

One morning when they woke up, Myrna said, "Okay, how much fun do we have to have today?"

They took it all in good spirits. They noticed that police and security personnel were much more present than they were in Minnesota.

"Do they think we might steal stuff? Myrna wondered.

"Well, yes, I guess so." I said, "When you live here awhile you just don't notice that anymore."

My brother Calvin and his wife Audrey also visited for a couple weeks with two of their three sons, Dan and Steve. A friend living nearby was kind enough to offer Dan and Steve a place to sleep so we avoided crowding our small apartment.

The third son, Chuck, the oldest, had visited us a few years before his parents and brothers arrived. Chuck and I took a city tour.

As we pulled up to the United Nations, a little kid on the bus with his parents, woke from a nap and sleepily said, "Which tallest building in the world is this one?"

You can get that way if you've been toured out but want to stay part of the program. Chuck decided to go off on his own one day and when he didn't come home when I thought he should, I became anxious and worried.

Bill had to remind me, "Carole, he's a grown man of 21. He can handle himself."

True, he was, and a smart, capable guy; but I could not put aside my feeling of responsibility for him. I did not relax until he came home.

I was glad that – except for my father – my whole family had been able to visit and experience our life in New York City.

Our bedroom was small with just barely room for the platform bed, a night table, and a TV stand. There were bookshelves on the wall and a metal cabinet at one end of the room. I remember being scared at night when we first moved in. I wasn't used to the sounds of the building. I kept thinking I heard something sinister. I even wished Bill wouldn't breathe so loudly when he slept because I might not be able to hear somebody trying to break in.

That fear finally disappeared after a while. I became so secure at last that I never worried at all. Unlike when I first came to live in Litchfield, I was very nervous thinking how easy it would be to invade my little house. That worry too subsided.

My friends in Minnesota could not quite figure out why I was, and still am, so security minded. I explained that in New York City your life and well being depended on being alert and watchful; after awhile that awareness becomes second nature.

The fourth room in our apartment we called the dressing room. Not big enough for a bedroom but space enough for a built-in closet as well as a large wooden wardrobe. A few books stood on shelves covering what had been the door to another apartment. Two dressers, a cabinet, a small desk, and two chairs were all that fit into this room.

Bill had many clothes which he kept in the closet. He had a habit of not wearing new clothes and keeping old ones forever. He always worried he would spill on the new clothes and he had a purpose for the old ones. I called his collection the "Bill Wendt Memorial Wardrobe." Some of his sports jackets dated to the Fifties.

He explained that he might need to provide his own costumes for a theatrical production and if it took place in the Fifties, he was ready.

On the other hand, I figured it was simple: He could not throw anything away. I hated shopping so the few outfits I had fitted just fine in the wooden wardrobe.

After he was diagnosed with mesothelioma, and he knew he was dying, he packed up his shirts to send to Minnesota. He discovered he had kept 64. I don't know where he had them stored. And that was just the shirts. There were sweaters, pants, jackets, and coats. Some I am sure he had never worn because he had not found an occasion important enough to risk spilling on them.

Our cat, Lili, was as much a member of the household as we were. She arrived one day when Bill found her wandering in the hallway; looking dirty and half starved. He was on his way out but stopped to pick her up and hand her to me. We decided we would clean her up, feed her and then turn her over to whoever takes stray cats.

Of course, we kept her. She became a personality and an important part of our little family. We immediately laid down the law: She was not to jump on the bed or climb up on the kitchen table.

The first night after she had been fed and watered and cleaned up, we closed the two louvered doors to the bedroom, hooked them shut, and laid down to sleep. There was an inch of space between the bottom of the partition and the floor. We watched as a furry paw reached under one of the louvers and pulled on it. Rattle, rattle. The hook held; the louvers would not open. But, Lili a determined kitten, persisted. Rattle, rattle, rattle. Over and over she tugged at it.

Finally, we couldn't stand it anymore, so we opened the doors. Lili slept on the bed from then on if she wished and she almost always wished. Next day, it was hot. Lili figured out that to lie on her back, legs splayed out on the top of the kitchen table was the best place to cool off. We laughed, isn't she cute? After that, she climbed on the table whenever she chose. But she never did it when it was set for a meal. Funny how she knew that. Maybe because I screamed NOOOOOOOOOOOOOOOO the first time she tried it. Never did it again.

Try typing or writing at the table and she was all over the place, sitting on your paper or nudging your hand as you tried to write. I never minded that. Nor did Bill.

Bill was gone a lot for his show business jobs. So Lili and I became close friends. Once I felt sad for some reason and was sitting in the dressing room crying quietly.

Lili had been sleeping in the living room but soon appeared at my feet looking up at me with what I could only call concern. I have since learned from other pet owners that their cat or dog has sensed distress and come to be near them.

Another time I was quite sick, with a bad cold and a high fever. I was lying on my back when Lili crept onto the bed to snuggle between my arm and my chest. It was very comforting. She had never done that before nor did she after I was well again.

There was a tiger under her calico fur. I once thought it would be a good idea to give her a change of scenery and carry her down three flights to get the mail. I was just turning the corner to open the front door when some sound alarmed her.

I suddenly was holding twenty flying needles as she scrambled off my shoulder, down my back, leapt to the floor, and raced back to the apartment door. The wild animal surfaced; it didn't matter that I was her beloved friend. No sir, she was off and I was as beloved as tree bark.

Back upstairs, she was waiting at the door. She sedately sauntered back into the apartment as if nothing had happened. I learned a lesson: Never carry a cat on your shoulder outside her comfort zone.

One day I saw her sitting like a cat sculpture on the window sill of the tiny bathroom. She looked so beautiful that I could not help being cozy with her.

I leaned close and said, "Look at the beautiful kitty. How lovely you look."

She stared unblinking into my eyes. Then, she raised her paw and socked me right in the middle of my forehead. Yes, socked. No claws. A punch. I was so surprised I reacted without thinking and socked her back. Not hard but it was a punch right in the middle of HER forehead.

We stared at each other for a second and then I walked away. What had happened? Two animals responding to each other. She probably didn't like my being so close, staring and wanted me out of her space.

I instinctively responded like an animal to her. Punch for punch. Not serious punching -- no damage done but a point was being made. Back up. Punch. Punch me I punch you back. Thump. Simple. No hard feelings.

A plumber once came to fix a leak. Lili was watching him from the dressing room, sitting on a bureau. The plumber was aware of her, staring fixedly at his every move.

Finally, he said to me, "Is that a real cat? Is it alive?"

I said, "Yes, she is so interested in what you are doing she just can't move. See? I'll call her name."

I said, "Lili, what are you doing?"

She blinked and turned to look at me and meowed.

The plumber said, "She was so still for so long I thought she might have been stuffed or something."

She had learned to meow on demand. It became a parlor trick to say, "Our cat talks. Watch." I'd point a finger at her and say, "Speak."

And she would meow. It amazed our friends. The speaking trick had evolved from when I played a game where I would pretend to shoot her. I'd point a finger and say "Lili, bang!"

One day she meowed back at me. After that, I omitted the 'bang" and just said, "Speak." And so, the talking trick was born.

I have her ashes with me in Minnesota. Maybe I will get another cat some day. Maybe. UPDATE: I FOUND ANOTHER CAT. KIKI ARRIVED ONE WINTER DAY. THIRTY YEARS AFTER LILI DIED.

WHEN THE AC WENT OUT

It was 94 degrees and humid. With exquisite timing my thirteen- year-old air conditioner decided to just stop dead. What? It was working fine three days ago.

I immediately thought: Darn, can this mean I have to get a new one? I did not want to do that. I don't like to shop EVER. So, there I was, - floundering around my living room, trying to solve the problem.

Call me sexist, but I figure anything electric or "techie"in nature is a man's job; they like that sort of thing and often know what to do.

I thought, "Who do I know who could figure this out."

Hmm. Okay, my brother Calvin residing in a Burnsville nursing home. He was a carpenter and knew a lot about fixing things. He asked me many questions and I said I had done all that: Check the plug in, examine the cords and the AC for flaws, done that. After debriefing, my brother said, "I guess you need a new AC." Dang.

I hate that. Takes so much time finding the right one to replace my old one, ordering it, waiting for delivery, getting someone to put it in the window and get rid of the old one. We all know that drill.

But, I was not giving up on my experts. I called another friend: he lives a few miles out of town.

He asked the same questions my brother did, then sighed and said, "Better get a new one. If the company you get it from won't set it up, I'll do that for you." That was nice.

Still persistent, I called a friend in Florida. He used to live near me and was always very eager to help people out. I described my problem, and he too, said, "Well, cut to the chase. Get a new one. Sorry."

I had one last hope. I'd left a message for another fellow who lives in town. He's a jack of all trades. He called back. Once again, I droned on about the AC. After a few questions, he said, "I'd better come over and look at it." So he did. He checked out the cords, the plug in, the overall condition of the AC and found it a puzzle. Couldn't figure out what was wrong. He then opened the front grate to inspect the filter (it was clean) and otherwise look it over on the inside. Nothing appeared to be wrong. He then folded the grate back in place but one side stuck. He slammed it hard with the heel of his hand to make it fit, and it did. At the same time, EUREKA, the AC started working. We were both amazed, open mouthed, and speechless.

I said, "I guess all it needed was a good sock in the face."

He, being sensible, said it wasn't a mystery. He figured something inside might have been out of place and his sock just put it back where it should have been.

Between you and me, I disagree, I think he has the magic touch.

By the way, the AC's been running fine ever since. It better or I'll get my friend to come over and sock it again.

A friend called me up a few days after I had told her about socking the AC. She said her fan stopped working -- so, following my lead, she socked it a good one. It started up and had been working ever since. Go figure.

I AM NOT A DOCTOR – THOUGH I TRY TO BE

I have to remind myself that I am not a doctor. All my life I've been interested in medicine and will diagnose anyone who presents me with symptoms -- whether they want me to or not.

I suppose it started when I was three years old and inhaled a peanut. I had to be rushed from our Grove City farm to the University of Minnesota. A doctor found the nut in my lung and removed it. I had to stay at the hospital for ten days to be sure I had no after effects from the experience.

My mother said when she came to get me I did not want to leave. I had fallen in love with the doctor and hung onto him for dear life. I do not remember any of this but I figure that's where my intense interest in medicine began.

I research every disease, ache, or pain that I – or anyone else I know – is suffering from. It's a kind of game for me. I diagnose myself and if I need a doctor to confirm my findings, I make an appointment. Most of the time I am right. They come up with the same result. I never tell them what I think I have so as not to prejudice their opinion.

One time though I was way way wrong. I found a lump on the top of my left thigh. I looked that up. I was horrified to discover that it could be cancer of the muscle which is very serious. I worried and worried.

During a routine appointment with my gynecologist a few days later, I asked her, trying not to reveal my terror, "Take a look at this. What is that?"

I held my breath as she reached out and rubbed the area.

"Oh, that," she said dismissively, "that's just fat."

She looked at me curiously when I laughed out loud at her diagnosis. It definitely wasn't cancer of the muscle. If it had been, by this time I would not be writing this or doing anything else.

I'm what some doctors hate: someone who knows enough medicine to be dangerous and yes, sometimes a pain in the butt. I ask a lot of questions about my own case but also about members of my family when they are ill. I'm the one who asks the doctor questions like: What's his hemoglobin? Have you checked for a UTI? What drugs have you prescribed? Could she have pneumonia? I find – as I am sure most doctors do -- that diagnosing is the most interesting and important part of medicine. It's like detective work.

I am so glad when I meet a doctor socially who likes to talk about their work. That can have some drawbacks: I had dinner with a surgeon several years ago. I ordered calf's brains and when my dish arrived, he pointed out the cerebrum, the medulla, and the cerebellum. Enlightening but not exactly stimulating to my appetite. Not to worry, I ate them with pleasure anyway.

VANITY, VANITY: DOES IT EVER END?

I don't know about you but I like to appear younger than I am. And, I also like to look nice. If someone guesses my age as less than it is, I am pleased.

My brother says, "You're OLD. Face it!"

NO, I refuse to face it. By the way, he isn't always so matter of fact about aging; he once asked me to check out a product that is supposed to get rid of bags under your eyes.

So, see? I'm not the only in the family who wants to look better. By the way, that product only works for about ten hours and the bags are back. Can you imagine people's amazement when the effect wears off and you age before their eyes?

I have come up with some tips on how to appear more youthful. One: Don't groan when you sit down or get up. That's a dead giveaway. It's hard to do that though when your knees ache a lot.

Two: Try to look nonchalant as you grab furniture or railings or banisters in order to walk about with confidence. And, a tip for women: If you feel shaky walking beside a fellow, take his arm. But act as though you are simply being friendly so as not to give away the fact that you might otherwise fall flat on your face.

If your friend is a woman, no problem; she was probably about to grab YOUR arm. Among us ladies, we are not so shy.

Three: As to walking slowly, which is now almost a requirement, make it a point to examine the sights along the way – that way you can take a break without seeming to be an old person who needs a rest stop.

Which I am, but I don't like to advertise. I will halt a walk to observe dogs, children, piles of colorful leaves, vintage cars, clouds, unusual houses, gardens, and cracks in the sidewalk. You get the point. You will be seen as a curious person, interested in all aspects of life – one who is living life to the fullest as opposed to a very senior citizen who can't get around so well anymore.

A theory among some psychologists is that ACTING happy can make you FEEL happy. I suggest that ACTING young, can you make you FEEL young. And young is good, right? You'll have to excuse me now, it's time for my nap, or, rather, time for meditating – with my eyes closed.

HELP IS ON THE WAY

I do not have children. Nor did my sister. Not so much on purpose -- it was the luck of the draw.

That means, unlike most of my peers in town, I do not have sons, grandsons, daughters, daughters in law, grand daughters and others of like rank, eager to do the odd chores around my place.

Calm down. I know you're going to say, "Wait a minute. My kids and other progeny live far away; they work full time even if they are close by. They aren't necessarily falling all over themselves to mow my lawn, fix my leaky roof, or move my refrigerator away from the wall so I can clean behind it."

Okay, okay, that might be true but here are some of the tasks my friends' offspring have helped them with: wallpapering the kitchen, hooking up the garden hose, carting the rider mower to the repairman – and that list goes on. Now, I am not jealous. My friends deserve such attentions. After all, they changed a lot of diapers, cooked a lot of meals, and worried themselves sick after the kids learned to drive and sometimes came home too late.

Here's the point: I have to have helpers who don't owe me anything. I have to win them over with a decent price for their services and, of course, a pleasing manner. That works out pretty well most of the time.

I have a great plumber – he responds so fast he's at my house before I've hung up the phone. (I exaggerate only a little.) I am not telling you who he is for fear you might win him away. My car mechanic is the best. Reliable and witty to boot. Both of these guys have excellent senses of humor. I got really lucky with them.

And, once in a while I need some sewing done: taking something in or hemming up slacks (I'm losing weight so that has become necessary lately). I do some of that myself but talk about amateurish, wow. So if it matters, I take it to my favorite seamstress in town. She is excellent at her job and a lively conversationalist besides.

But some disappointments occur too. One fellow promised he'd show up to help me out and did not. One promised an estimate on a big job three years ago and I'm still waiting. Another ignored about half a dozen calls until I finally got the hint and realized he just was not interested. Happens to all of us, I am sure.

Generally, I have had very good luck finding help for stuff my nonexistent sons and daughters might have done for me. On the other hand, my progeny might have decided to live in France working for the United Nations, become movie stars and always on location, or philosophers living in the Outback of Australia.

You never know. You just play it as it lays – fend for yourself – and if you get lucky, you might find gems like those I found.

FROM SOLITAIRE TO PHILOSOPHY

Okay, now don't judge me. I have been playing a lot of solitaire on the internet. I know that's nothing to be proud of. I could be doing good works in the community. I get it. Nevertheless, through this rather pointless activity, I have learned a lot.

I am now capable of always winning the "easy" level of solitaire offered by Microsoft. Every game is different but I never lose anymore. Once in a while I move to harder games, and I do win at those too – sometimes -- but not always.

Now, here's the thing: I have learned that I prefer to win ALL THE TIME at an easy game rather than play a more difficult game at which I sometimes lose. Get the message?

Lesson learned: I hate to lose, at anything. I remember as a kid staging a tantrum if I lost at a game. Not proud of that but you get the point. I recall almost destroying a tennis racket (given to me by Billie Jean King, whom I had interviewed for the Today show). Why was I ready to demolish that valuable racquet? Because I had lost a game. (I know, nuts!) Once I find a way to win, I stick with it. Which may explain why I stayed married for life – forty years -- until my husband passed away. Why I lived in the same Manhattan apartment for over 50 years; it was rent controlled and a winner. And, why I stayed in the same job at NBC for over 30 years.

And, that's probably why I came back to live in Litchfield in my grandparents', and parents' former home. Sticking to what works runs in the family, I guess.

So, you see, mindless games on the internet can be enlightening –even though they may reveal a character trait that isn't necessarily attractive. But aren't we encouraged to know ourselves? As Polonius says to his son Laertes in Hamlet, "… to thine own self be true; and it must follow as the night the day, thou canst not then be false to any man."

I am definitely not a gambler. I stick to what works. However, that means I may not take a risk that later I wonder if I should have taken. But in the end I go with Harry Truman, who, when asked if he regretted dropping the atomic bomb on Japan, said that he made the best decision he could make given the time within which he had to make it and given the information he had at the time. He said he had no regrets, ever. Hurray for Harry.

That made sense to me and still does. I say, learn from the past but never regret it – If you did your research and made the best decision you knew how to make within the time period you had to make it, you can't blame yourself if it doesn't turn out the way you wanted it to. That gets rid of the "if only" blues.

I now beg your indulgence for having lectured a bit. I am a very senior citizen and maybe I do know something by now.

Class dismissed.

FALLING LEAVES

Will someone tell me why we have to rake leaves? They fall in the woods all the time and no one says we have to rake the woods.

According to my guru, Google, leaves can protect tiny animals (bugs, worms and such) who live underneath them. Unless you have a very very thick layer of leaves, the advice is don't worry about it, the lawn will survive. Of course, you could mow those leaves and make mulch out of them. That's considered better than raking.

Of course, there is the aesthetic reason for getting rid of leaves. Our natural bent for manipulating nature inclines us to like a neat look with leaves gone and bare grass showing. But, it turns out raking is not a requirement for the health of your yard though it might get you the approval of your neater neighbors.

I do have a pocket in my yard that accumulates an alarming pileup of leaves. It's a sheltered area that lies between houses and close to three trees. It attracts every leaf in Meeker County. I swear I've seen a few stray palm tree leaves in the mix. Okay, so I'm exaggerating. But not by much.

That space can get so thick it could smother the grass eventually, so, I guess my work there is probably required.

There I'll be, that white haired lady stumbling around corralling leaves into huge oversize trash bags. If I were sure I could get up again, I'd sit on them and squash them down so I could get more leaves into each bag. Maybe I can persuade a more limber friend to do that for me.

"Yeah," I'd say, "just fall on that bag over there, squash it down so I can get more leaves into it. Go ahead, it'll be fun."

That would work. Any takers?

AUTUMN: SIGNS OF TIME PASSING

Some people have watch dogs; I have watch leaves. I am alerted any time someone comes to my door by the loud crunching of the leaves on my deck.

At first I thought I should sweep the deck clean but every time I did the leaves flew right back. They just love that deck. I knew I had mail the other day when I heard crunching on the deck. That's useful I figured, so I am leaving them until the first snowfall. That way I'll always know I have visitors before they even ring the bell.

Autumn has other charms. I like yellow and red trees popping up everywhere. I have a young tree in my yard that blushed furiously when the weather first turned cool. A grown up tree across the street is reddening up slowly, the color starting on the outside and moving in toward the trunk. I remember that maple from when it was a little punk and now it's 45 feet tall.

I've only been living full time in Minnesota for a few years so I'm still not used to all these leaves on the ground. I have a small lot with twelve trees on it so they really pile up – in some places at least two feet deep. Walking through them is like wading through corn flakes. I like kicking them around.

Autumn is pretty but it does make a person melancholy. It seems as if everything is dying. Really not though, mostly, it's not death it's hibernation. Time for me to stock up on good books and food, check out some movies on DVD, and figure out how to entertain myself when I go into hibernation too. I'm not a good one for driving in snow and ice so I know I'll be spending more time at home.

The Israelis once produced a musical called "To Live another Summer." In their country that's a challenge for all ages. For me and my older friends -- as time goes by -- "to live another summer" becomes more meaningful.

I don't feel old most of the time until I hear about a friend who has died, or has been diagnosed with terminal cancer, or needs a pacemaker, or can't walk unassisted. If I lived like a hermit and knew nothing about anyone else's health, aging would only be obvious to me at times, aches and pains when I get up in the morning and that darn left knee that hurts now and then. Otherwise, I go about my business as usual -- with a few more rest breaks thrown in.

A slower pace – that's the thing these days. It doesn't feel like I am getting older – as autumn reminds me – it feels more like it's time to take it easy. And I do. Works for me. So far.

THE AFTERMATH

I was out in my garage the other day sorting through my late sister's property. I was sad and distracted as I separated what I would keep and what I would discard. Covid 19 took her life three weeks after she tested positive. She was 82.

I was glad of the distraction of settling her affairs; keeping busy prevented me from despair.

Still, in the middle of sad doings, there always arises times for laughter. Myrna was witty and loved a good joke – even in the face of tragedy. Her husband, Marvin, was like her in that way. We were driving back from St. Cloud after Marvin's appointment with his oncologist. It had been a grim interview at which we learned Marvin faced a long battle with leukemia. The disease eventually killed him a year later.

On that day Marvin was alone in the back seat of the car when he suddenly sneezed loudly. "Well," he said, "at least THAT works!" Our laughter dispelled the gloomy mood of the moment.

Back to my sad job of sorting Myrna's things. In the middle of my work, I realized I could not find my glasses. I vaguely remembered taking them off, outdoors. But why did I do that? Where did I put them? A mystery. So annoying.

Then, I remembered Saint Anthony of Padua, the saint who finds things. Very seldom have I asked for his help – only for very important lost objects – car keys, etc. He always came through. This time lost glasses qualified for his assistance. So, I asked for it.

Meanwhile, I emptied the garbage can and went through everything in it. Nothing. I searched the garage. Nothing. I went inside the house and sulked. Come on, Saint Anthony, help me, I thought. As I looked out the window, I saw something shining in the sun on the ground near the garbage can. What? A piece of glass? Can it be? I raced outside and there they were -- my glasses. How could I not have seen them? I searched that space thoroughly minutes before. I picked them up. One earpiece was bent at a 90 degree angle, the frame was broken and one lens fell out in my hand. I must have stomped on them hard or driven over them. I was a little disappointed in Saint Anthony's help this time. I silently chided him for returning them to me so damaged.

His response came to me, "Ayy, I find'em, I don't fix 'em.'"

Remember Saint Anthony is Italian. I wonder: Is there a saint who fixes things?

I so wish Myrna were here so I could tell her that story; she'd have loved it. And that's the worst of it; losing her laughter.

A MINNESOTA WALKABOUT

In Australia, a young boy becomes a man by going on "Walkabout" – an Aborigine rite of passage. The boy strikes out into the Outback, the Australian wilderness. He must survive on his own for several months, armed only with a spear. If he makes it back alive, he has passed the test for becoming a man.

My walkabout was not quite like that but it was also a very special journey. No spear was involved and most of it was by car. So, perhaps it needs to be called a Driveabout.

It began like this: Amanda, the Activity Director at my brother's nursing home in Burnsvlle, told me, since he and I were now fully vaccinated against COVID, I could at last take him for a car tour. That was something we both loved to do before Covid interfered lo those many months ago. And so began our version of a walkabout, or rather our driveabout.

In the car, we were armed –not with spears – but with a pound of grapes for munchies, a jug of water, paper towels, a large dish towel for a bib and a collapsible wheel chair in the trunk. We were ready for almost everything.

Off we went. Calvin wanted to visit a gazebo we had discovered when he lived in an assisted living apartment in Anoka. He had often said he wished he could see that place again. Now, after two years away from Anoka, he was going to do just that.

The gazebo is set in a tiny park on the shore of the Mississippi alongside a most excellent swing. We sat in the gazebo and watched Ol' Man river for awhile. I sat in the swing for a few minutes. It was just swell but then the cool breeze off the river began to feel chilly so we got ready to leave – but not before I placed a small rock in an obscure location to record our visit. We plan to add a rock every time we go there, which we definitely will.

We next made a quick stop at River Oaks apartments, where Calvin had lived before moving to Burnsville. Then we moved on to Coon Rapids where he and his late wife Audrey had made their home for years. Health issues forced them to sell. The buyer was a young man. He later wrote a kind letter to thank them for letting him buy their lovely home. The letter was so touching, Calvin said "it made Audrey cry."

The day was truly a sentimental journey for Calvin. The Coon Rapids house was their first and only home where they had raised their three sons. I pulled into the driveway and knocked on the door. It was a Sunday afternoon and the young man was home. I explained who I was and that Calvin was in the car. With that, the young man, Bryan, immediately stepped outside with his mask on and barefoot. I was surprised he didn't put shoes on.

He said, "I'm okay. It's not that cold." He told Calvin he hadn't had to make many changes, that he house was in good condition. He said he was soon to marry and planned to raise his family in the home where Calvin had raised his family. As we drove away, Calvin was moved by knowing that a new young family would enjoy the home he and Audrey had loved so much.

And, now it was time for some snacks. We were just down the road from Calvin's favorite McDonald's. He had hoped his friend, the manager, would be on duty; but no, it was Sunday and she was at home. We ordered two quarter pounders and coffee to take to the car. No eating indoors was their policy. Fine with us, we were prepared with all our supplies. We were very hungry and those burgers really hit the spot.

Calvin leaned back in his seat, heaved a sigh, and said, smiling in the sunshine, "This has been a perfect day."

And off we went back to Burnsville. I brought his wheel chair to him and helped him into the lobby where he was greeted cheerfully by the nurse on duty.

I said, "Do you need me to get you to your room?" "Oh, no," he said, "I can take it from here."

And, after that perfect day, I thought we could both "take it from here."

I drove 255 miles over a 12 hour day. To my amazement, I did not feel tired at any point – during or after our "driveabout."

In fact, I felt revived – still do.

UPDATE: Calvin passed away before we could place another stone at the gazebo. It is my plan to do so as soon as I can.

GOOD SAMARITANS LIVE!!

My sister and I were cruising along on a nice smooth highway. It was 92 outside but we were nice and cool because I had just gotten the air conditioning fixed.

Then, unbelievably, the car just slowed down and stopped. What? I turned it off. Started it again; it ran a few seconds and stopped. Hey, it's never done this before. It wasn't overheated; the oil had just been changed; there was enough gas. What's the deal? Could it be the air conditioning unit malfunctioning?

Only my mechanic can know and he isn't here. Now what? At least ten miles south of Willmar, 30 miles from home. It was Memorial Day weekend; a Saturday.

I raised my hand and the first car that came by stopped. It was a small red car that shone in the bright sunshine; the driver was a Latino fellow who barely spoke English.

I said, "May I borrow your cell phone?"

"Yes," he said handing it over.

I found I needed him to punch the buttons because I could not read the tiny numbers and letters on the thing. He carefully punched in the number for Triple A. I waited. A woman came on and slowly took down the details. Ten miles south of Willmar on highway 71. Okay, someone will be there within the hour. The Latino man drove off after shyly refusing any money for his trouble.

While I was using his phone, two Latino men in a silver sedan made a U turn and came by to ask if we needed any more help.

"Thanks, no," I said and they drove off.

We waited. The heat was almost lethal, coupled as it was with a strong dry wind from the south. We were getting hotter and hotter; we drank our diet Pepsi. My sister was worried about heatstroke. So was I. After all, we are Scandinavians and over 80. Seemed things could get bad. Then, another car stopped. A middle aged couple in a van.

"Okay?" "Oh, yes, thanks." They moved on.

Another car made a U turn and stopped. "Need help?"

"We have a tow truck coming."

"Okay," they drove on.

Immediately, another car pulled up. Out jumped a young man in a tuxedo. He was happy.

I asked, "Are you a musician?"

"No, just came from a wedding. Need help?"

"No, thanks. A truck's on the way. Was it your wedding?"

"No, a friend's."

"Thanks, but don't worry," I said. "We have a truck coming."

By now, we'd waited about half an hour and we were getting very uncomfortable. A fellow in a van stopped after making a U turn. Bearded, glasses, a bright smiling guy. He turned out be a farmer in the area. We learned he also had a house in Spicer on Green Lake.

"Oh, a rich farmer, eh?" my sister teased.

"Oh, no, investment property," he said, not wanting to be considered well- heeled. He left after being assured we were okay.

He had no more than turned away when another helper stopped. A sleek sports car convertible with a vanity plate: Just two letters. The middle aged man was dressed fashionably; white T shirt and well tailored summer pants. He wore a smoothly combed white haired toupee. Almost looked real. Big smile with well capped snow white teeth.

"Are you a Senator?" I asked.

"Oh, no," he said.

"Well, that license plate with just two initials on it suggests an important person."

"Oh, those are my late wife's initials. I bought that car for her and she died 8 months later."

"My sister and I have recently lost our husbands so we can certainly sympathize."

"Need any help here?"

"Oh, no, thanks," I said and made the "truck's on the way" speech.

He said he was 1600 miles from his home in Edmonton, Canada. He'd come south to attend a friend's wedding. He told us his profession was finding out about fraudulent companies.

He testified in Washington against Enron.

"That can be dangerous work," he said.

About now, I figured out he wanted to talk, a lot. Lonely guy, I imagine. But, he finally wished us well and left.

We were now so frustrated that when another couple stopped, I asked to use their cell phone. I told triple A to call the tow truck company and tell them to hurry up before we had heatstroke.

She said, elderly heat-stricken women or no, she wasn't allowed to nag them. The couple had a cool, air conditioned van and offered to let my sister sit with them to relieve her discomfort.

I said, "Why not drive her to the Holiday Inn in Willmar and I can wait for the truck and pick her up?"

And so she got in their van and zoomed to town. I waited for another ten minutes. I decided to take a chance and start the car. Eureka! It started and did not act like it would quit on me. Slowly, and then faster and faster I raced back to Willmar. Never saw a tow truck headed my way. The car was working fine; but I did not dare turn on the air conditioner. I met Sis at the Holiday Inn; we had a great Cobb salad, and drove on home to Litchfield. I figured there was something wrong with the car, probably the newly repaired air-conditioner is malfunctioning and yet, the mechanic could not find anything wrong with it and it never acted up again.

Despite our discomfort and frustration, it turned out to be a good day. Seven cars stopped; ten people expressed concern and three provided help with patience and kindness, refusing the money we offered.

Very reassuring to learn that. In the process we had some interesting conversations. Strangers caring about strangers –nice to be reminded of that.

FLAG REMINDER

I stood outside the Litchfield library the other day. The wind was whipping about, even making me sway a bit.

I looked up at the flag; it was blown straight out in the high wind, fluttering fast. The stars and stripes were beautiful against the bright blue sky.

I am not a particularly sentimental person but it lifted my heart to see it there. Rising above, flying in the breeze.

For some reason, I thought about Allen Peterson, my cousin, who was shot dead after fighting his way across France and into Belgium. He was part of the D-Day invasion. He had just turned 19 when he died. He lies at Lake Ripley Cemetery.

I thought how many people have given so much to preserve what that beautiful flag stands for.

So many people have pledged allegiance to it -- people of all opinions, who have argued passionately – and sometimes dangerously. Yet I like to think all those combatants agree on one thing: Love of country. All struggling to show their allegiance in their own way and at the same time trying to come to some agreement on how to do so together.

This country was founded by smart, flawed, ambitious men and women. It's inhabited by pioneers, immigrants, and immigrants' descendants. Some came against their will.

All, for their own reasons, came with rebellion in their hearts. Rebellion is in our DNA. For good or ill, we resist orders, question authority, and strive to go our own way independently. That has worked to our strength and our weakness.

Figuring out the difference is no easy task. Yet, we keep at it. And for the sake of cousin Allen and his fellow men and women who died for us, I hope we continue to keep at it.

MY NEW CRUSH: HOUDINI, THE CAT

One day while sightseeing in the country, I stopped by a new friend's house. Karen lives on a lovely farm in a beautiful home. We became acquainted when she joined a club I belong to. Karen is a widow and lives with a friend I was soon to meet.

Her living room was huge. Windows lined one wall and sunshine flooded the place. We had just begun to talk when I noticed a large black cat staring at me from the window sill across the room.

I love cats; I still miss Lili, my calico cat, who died after being my roommate for 21 years.

"Who is that?" I asked.

Karen said, "That's Houdini. He's rather standoffish; doesn't take to strangers very well. He is not particularly friendly to me either. But I love him anyway."

By this time, Houdini had leaped down from the window sill and, eyeing me watchfully, began to edge nearer. Cat people know how to behave when strange cats check you out. Sit very still, lower your hand and let them sniff you to see who you are, all the while you murmur in a high baby voice, "Here, kitty, kitty. I am a friend. You are beautiful. What a wonderful cat you are." Houdini, to Karen's and my delight, approached me, sniffed my hand, and let me lightly touch his tail as he strode away.

Karen was amazed. "He's never come that close to a stranger before. Even with me, he'll sit in my lap once in a while but only for a few minutes."

I said maybe he approached me because he sensed I was a cat in a previous life. Maybe in ancient Egypt where they worshiped cats and even mummified them -- burying them alongside the pharaohs.

I toured Egypt once and brought back a tiny statue of Bastet, a black cat ancient Egyptians believed to be a god. Oh, I am definitely fascinated by cats.

Karen and I chatted later on the phone. She said, 'Houdini kept watching the door after you left; I know he was wondering what happened to the nice lady. He also jumped up on the sofa where you had been sitting. He seemed to be searching for you. He's never done that before."

I was flattered that Houdini had taken a liking to me, but I sensed it would be a good idea to allay any fears Karen might have that Houdini would like me better than her.

"Karen," I told her, "I'd never want to compete with you for his affection – hard as that would be to do."

"Oh, that's okay," she said. "Don't worry about that even though I guess I am a little sensitive on that score. We had a dog that preferred my husband to me – even though I fed him, brushed him and took care of him. One day when I was coming up the driveway in our pickup truck, the dog greeted me -- running alongside the truck, barking and jumping. But when I got out, and he saw it was me not my husband, his face dropped, he stopped barking and jumping and ran off. Now that can hurt your feelings." She laughed at herself but I could see it was still a painful memory.

Karen said she'd love for us to get together again sometime. We had a lot in common: both widows, both avid readers, and both, not antisocial, but happy to be independent and living on our own.

I said,"Yes, let's do that. Love to see Houdini again" and I added quickly, "you too, of course."

Karen got the joke. Happily, she has a sense of humor. I wonder if Houdini has a sense of humor too. He seemed rather serious. We shall see.

Karen advised me to get another cat. She thinks I need one. I think she may be right -- my crush on Houdini a case in point.

UPDATE: A few years later, I found Kiki, then a kitten, shivering in my yard one freezing February afternoon. A lucky day.

GHOSTING AROUND THE HOUSE

I don't sleep through the night. I seem to have to get up and roam the house at odd hours -- often sometime around 3 AM I have done that since I was a kid. Usually, I wake up to read. I remember on the farm when we had no electricity and used lamplight. (Yes, I go back a ways.) My Dad also read late at night. I wasn't supposed to be up at night but I wanted to read too.

So, I would sneak out to the hallway and hold my book up to catch the faint light from my Dad's lamp. My mother caught me and worried I wouldn't get enough sleep. I was a growing child, after all.

She consulted our country doctor who asked, "Is she healthy?"

"Yes," she said.

"Well, then," he said, "Leave her alone. Let her read."

And she did. My mother was an avid reader, too, so I figure she sympathized. That created my habit of roaming the house at night. I discovered that my mother walked around at night too as did my sister. I suppose it ran in the family – at least among the women -- my father and my brother slept soundly through the night.

It all came to a head one night years after my sister and I had homes of our own. We were visiting my mother for a few days when one night about 2 or 3 AM, we discovered that all three of us were drifting about in the dark in our nightgowns, moving from bathroom to kitchen to living room. We slipped by each other and did not speak because we did not want to wake up completely and not be able to go back to sleep. I know, sounds goofy, but it worked.

We came to call it "ghosting" as that's what it seemed to be. We were like sleepwalking Lady Macbeths. Only we were not compelled to wash our hands incessantly and mutter, "Will these hands ne'er be clean?" We just looked for a piece of cake, or a book, or a movie magazine and then drift back to bed and almost immediately fall back to sleep.

When I visit friends, I have to warn them I might "ghost" about their houses too. And not just to stop in the bathroom. I might examine the pictures on their walls, check out their libraries, look through their magazines, or play with their cat, always entertaining. Cats ghost about at night too -- which is why I am pretty sure I was a cat in another life.

Don't look at me that way, millions of people believe in reincarnation. In fact, one survey showed that one in four Americans believe in reincarnation. Who'd have thought? I'm thinking I might have been a big cat, a black panther, maybe. Don't you love it? Nothing like a fantasy to lighten the day.

FIRST LOVE

Don't underestimate the maturity of teenagers. They sometimes know exactly what they want and make decisions that last a lifetime and turn out to be the right choice.

She was 15; he was 16. They started paying attention to each other at the ice skating rink across from their high school. They were both good students; getting high grades in all their classes.

She rode to school on the bus because she lived too far away to walk. He lived in town with what was known to be a troubled family. They began to date and soon were going steady, telling each other they were in love.

It was usual for teenagers at that time to go steady; in fact, several such couples married not long after graduation from high school. Soon, everyone knew they were going steady too. A teacher told her she was a good influence on him and was glad they were going together. That information didn't thrill the girl; she felt it demeaned him and gave her too much responsibility. Does anyone really like being the best thing that ever happened to another person? She didn't.

They were new at this love game confessing to one another they'd never been in love before, the way the stories told it. A photograph of them at that time showed them standing awkwardly together; his arm around her shoulder, she gazing into the camera unsmilingly.

Even in the black and white picture, it's clear he is blushing. She remembered that many years later when she came across the picture in an old album.

They went to the prom together. He in a scratchy wool suit; she in a long dress she held up with both her hands when her mother posed them for a picture. They looked so innocent and they were, in those days before the Pill and the permissive Sixties.

There were no flaws in their yearlong romance, but then, it ended abruptly. Half a sentence was all it took.

They were sitting in the car he borrowed from his aunt. His arm around her. He leaned close and said, . "When we get married – "

She stopped him, "I'm not getting married – ever – to anyone. I'm sorry but I can't."

He was shocked. "What do you mean? We've

been going steady for a year; we love each other. Why can't we get married?"

"Because I have things to do, places to go. I can't do that and be married."

To her amazement, he began to cry. And then, she did too. But it didn't change her mind.

They never spoke to each other again from that moment on. She kept track of him. Later, they were married, but not to each other.

She did what she wanted to do; she went places and did things. He did what he wanted to do. He settled down and had children. For several years, it went well for him but then came a divorce and a daughter's suicide. He declined into alcoholism and isolated himself. Then, cancer killed him.

She never regretted her decision -- even felt relieved she hadn't changed her mind. Otherwise, would she now be a divorcee and the mother of a suicide? She wondered. Or, would his life have been better with her? Does any one of us really save anyone else? Or do our lives play out inevitably no matter who accompanies us?

He had once said to her father, "I never should have let her get away."

It probably soothed his ego to think he could have stopped her. She smiled when her father told her what he had said.

"But you know, don't you, Daddy, no one could have stopped me."

"Oh, yes," he said, "I knew that but I let him think what he wanted to think."

THE CAT KNOWS

My calico cat, Lili, always wanted me to quit smoking. Here's how I know this: If I were sitting at the kitchen table reading or writing, she would jump into my lap. The first time she caught me smoking she narrowed her eyes, shook her head, and immediately jumped right back down.

After that, she would come and sit on the floor looking up at me seated at the table. I'd look at her, show her my cigarette and say, "I'm smoking."

She would turn away and walk out of the room. If I showed her my hands, and said, "It's okay, I'm not smoking." She would leap up to sit on my lap. I finally learned my lesson and quit that evil habit.

Lili taught me how to move gracefully. Cats don't walk, they glide. They don't plop themselves down for a nap; they slowly settle into a bonelessly relaxed position.

Lili would be so completely laid out on the bed it seemed as though she had been dropped from a great height to almost melt into the quilt. She would appear to be unconscious in deep sleep but when I whispered her name, she'd give herself away by lifting the tip of her tail.

"Ah ha," I'd say, "you heard me; don't pretend to be asleep."

And her tail would lift again. Once in a while, she would slowly open her eyes, gaze at me, and then slowly shut them again. That's what is known as a "cat kiss." Sometimes, I would go first, slowly closing my eyes and she would then return my "kiss."

I lived with Lili for 21 years. We spent a lot of time together. My husband traveled; we lived in a small Manhattan apartment. The cat never went outside so we became pals.

I learned to move smoothly. I learned that cats do not like quick movements; it upsets them. When the phone rang, I did not leap up and race to answer it. I would slowly stand and walk to the phone. Lili would have been startled otherwise. Loud noises also bothered her. I learned to speak in a modulated tone. However, I did use loud noises to train her. If she did something I did not want her to do, such as leap onto the kitchen table, I shouted loudly, NO. She hated that and immediately leapt down. She learned her lesson.

One never hits a cat. Unlike dogs, cats do not forgive and forget. I never called her to me for anything but what she would like. If she needed to go to the vet, which she hated, I would pick her up quickly and put her into her carrying case before she knew what was going on.

I would not call her for that. She knew when I did call her, it meant good food, good television (more on that later), or something else I knew she would want to see, do, or eat.

I learned patience from my cat. Even when she knew it would be good to come when called, it was still absolutely required in cat culture that she make me wait at least 30 seconds before responding. No amount of calling changed that.

Contrary to what some folks think, cats are sympathetic animals. Once, I sat weeping at my desk. I forget now why. I looked down and there sat Lili at my feet looking straight up into my eyes. I had not called her. She had been asleep in the bedroom. Was she being sympathetic? Seemed to me she was. It definitely was unusual behavior.

Once, I was quite sick with a miserable cold and laid out on my bed. Lili -- in another unusual move -- laid herself along my side between my arm and my chest.

She snuggled there for a long time. It was quite comforting. She got up to have a bite to eat and then came right back to her vigil beside me. Later,

I learned nursing home cats can often be found on the beds of dying residents. In fact, in an eerie fashion, the cats have predicted deaths by settling themselves next to patients not known to be dying but who subsequently did pass away.

I said I would talk about her television habits. The first time she noticed a TV set, I was on the floor scraping wax off the linoleum (don't ask.) I had a small TV beside me to entertain myself. Lili came walking over to see what I was up to when a close-up of a bear's head came on the screen.

Lili froze in amazement and then cautiously crept around behind the TV to find out where the bear came from. I realized Lili and I shared an interest in nature shows. She especially liked programs about lions, chimpanzees, and birds. I watched TV in the bedroom and when a show I knew she'd like came on, I would call her to me.

Then, I'd tap the screen to show her where to look. One program was so fascinating she watched for about 20 minutes. I knew she was following the action as she moved her head from one side to the other. I have photos to prove this by the way. She did not like commercials; they would break her concentration and she would stop watching. I hate ads too so if we watched together, it was always public TV we tuned in to. She had good taste.

Give it a shot; try watching TV shows your cat likes. You could do worse.

WHAT'S WITH MY WINDOW SHADES?

The other day my kitchen window shade just fell on the floor. What the heck? It wasn't anything I did. True: The shade just barely fits into its little hooks; it's almost too short but, come on, no need to just take a dive. So, I shoved some balled-up duct tape beside the hook to make it stick out more from the wall and put the shade back up. The tighter fit held and I'm hoping the problem is solved.

Next, I raised the shade in another room and the bottom ripped almost completely off. That stick that is inserted across the bottom of the shade? Just tore right off; hanging by only a couple inches. Out came my faithful transparent duct tape. I laid the shade on my kitchen table, carefully repaired it and got it back up. But, first I had to wait for the sun to move. When I first looked, the sunlight blinded me so badly I couldn't see to do the job.

Hold on, the shades weren't done revolting. Another shade in the same room suddenly just popped off its hooks. Was it showing solidarity with the other rebels? Did I bump it somehow? As I lifted my arms to investigate the problem, the curtain fell off its hooks too. Hey, I cry foul -- that's overdoing it. I completely removed both curtain and shade. And, without too much fuss, got them both back up. Duct tape not necessary. I guess it just needed some TLC from the landlady.

Do extra cold temperatures make shades and curtains want to leave home? Or at least make a fuss? Don't tell me they don't have minds of their own. This was a coordinated insurrection. I'm not quite sure what the point of it was -- other than to get some attention. Okay, okay, they got some attention. Next, I suppose the light bulbs will blow out.

MY LILAC BUSH AND ME

I wonder how my lilac bush likes living with me. I water it from time to time and trim its branches a little bit. Since I put up the bird house and hung suet from two of its branches, it's been home to dozens of residents. Some just fly through but many hang out in it regularly. I have seen mostly blackbirds, wrens, sparrows, a blue jay or two, several robins, and what might have been a nuthatch.

Does the bush like all this bird action? If she were human, would it feel like having bees, flies, or fleas buzzing about in her hair? (I've decided the lilac bush is female – never mind why.) Or do all her feathered visitors feel good to her?

And what does she think about life around her? Did she approve of all that new gravel I put down on my driveway right next to her? The gravel covered up bits and pieces of cement leftover from when my grandfather covered the driveway over 100 years ago. The bush had only known the old driveway – big change. It had also witnessed the felling of one old tree nearby and the addition of two new ones. I'm sure this year was a trial for her

– it being so dry- her blossoms looked a bit anemic. I'm sure she was embarrassed by the poor showing of blooms. Still, they smelled as sweet as ever. Maybe she's annoyed with me not doing enough to help her produce better blooms. She's probably right, I could have watered and fertilized more. But, I'm relying on her extensive root system after all these years to save the day and that next spring she will be covered in lush lilac flowers.

My lilac tree also had a hard time pushing out its gorgeous white blossoms; they ended up looking rather anorexic. This, in spite of the fact I watered and fertilized that tree a lot. So, you never know.

The lilac tree is a child. The lilac bush on the other hand is definitely a *grande dame*; I figure she is at least 80 years old. These days, as I say, she's the gathering place for dozens of flittering feathered folk who like to race in and out of her branches. The action is so fascinating a huge crow has occasionally stationed himself high up in the tree next to the bush. He appears to be taking notes. Is he planning to grab one of those little birds? Do crows eat meat? Wait a minute, of course, they like road kill, don't they?

I am watching closely to prevent any kind of

murderous mayhem in my yard. I'm betting on the tiny birds; they are ever- alert and fast as lightning.

But wait, maybe not so alert. One day I noticed a chickadee pecking at the rubber weather stripping around my windshield. He was so intent I was able to approach within a few feet of him. Unusual to get so close.

Suddenly, he looked up and I swear I heard him gasp and immediately slammed away as fast as his little whirring wings could take him.

Eating weather stripping? I looked closely. No embedded seeds, nothing worth eating. If I'd been a crow, he'd have been a goner.

I think he spread the word though, since his experiment in eating weather stripping, he must have told his fellows, don't go there. The food's no good and you could get eaten by a crow – or by whatever that big monster was that got too close to me.

MY COMPUTER HAS A WILL OF ITS OWN

The hills are alive for Julie Andrews; likewise, my computer is alive for me. I think it has a sense of humor. A rather mischievous one. The other day a very valuable file disappeared. It contained notes I had taken during a conference with a friend who had told me all the uses for baking soda, outside of for baking. You'd be surprised at how many ways it can be helpful -- whitening your teeth for starters.

But it's not baking soda we are going to get into here, but my computer shenanigans that bear examination. When I lost my file, I was very very upset. I had put a lot of work into typing up the scribbled notes I had made of what my baking soda expert told me. I looked into the "recycle bin" – not there. I checked my documents file over and over. It did not show up.

I called my computer expert; he told me to do something I could not figure out. I could have called him again but I did not want to reveal my inability to follow his instructions. I told myself maybe that file was not so important after all. I had printed a copy of it but I had wanted to preserve it in my documents file. I shrugged and decided to forget it.

It wasn't long after I resigned myself to its loss when my computer stopped torturing me. I did one last search for old time's sake, and lo! There it was. Bright as a penny, staring right back at me, the file itself, title correct, and in the right place.

Come on, you have to admit that there is something funny going on here. Now I have asked a supermarket employee to find the prune juice for me and she points to the shelf in front of me. Which I had stared at and didn't see. So, I grant you I might be at fault for not seeing what was in front of me on my screen, but I don't think so.

I think my computer likes fooling me. I swear I heard the faint sound of a snicker when I found the file. Don't give me that look; some computers can beat experts at chess. I'm just saying.

MY COCKEYED LAMP AND MY PERSISTENT POINSETTIA

Meet my roommates: my cockeyed lamp and my persistent poinsettia. I don't know why that kitchen lamp on the wall keeps tilting to the right side. No earthquakes near here; no work being done on the house to make it shift – so what's the deal?

Maybe it's just bored and wants a new outlook. I sure do. I would say one result of Covid isolation could account for my looking on a lamp and a plant as roommates. Don't look at me like that; don't tell me you've never talked to your car. Come on.

And that poinsettia. I bought it two Christmases ago for about five dollars. Tiny thing. The plastic green pot contains maybe 2/3 of a cup of dirt. Yet, that stubborn little thing keeps reaching for the sun. I water it faithfully but that's all the care it gets. Mostly, it's on its own. It had bright red leaves the first Christmas but not since. I have to admire its grit. I notice the stem has gotten very thick and strong. Looks like it's decided to live, by gum, and I'd better not try to push it around.

I often name things I like but I haven't named the lamp and the plant, yet. I named my alarm clock "Chuck."

Seemed appropriate; "Chuck" connotes sturdy and reliable. Like my nephew Chuck. My car is "The Lady Caroline." I figure if I flatter her with a title and give her my favorite's aunt's name, she'll be good to me. And so far, that's worked.

How about Lydia the Lamp and Punky the poinsettia? Works for me. I think that captures their personalities.

Update: No more poinsettias for me now that I have a cat that might want to champ on one. Research tells me poinsettias can make cats sick. Lilies are worse; they can even kill a cat. Word to the wise: Be careful with plants if you have pets that can get near them.

CAUGHT WITH MY HOSE DOWN

The first snowfall one year was right on schedule but I still got caught with my hose on the ground. I had to rip it out of five inches of snow to get it back into the garage for the season.

But at least I had the sense to get my swings, chairs, and tables stored away in time and covered up with various old tablecloths and bedspreads. I had that much foresight. And, I also put the window back in that north door where I had put a screen in the spring. Oh, and covered my air conditioner with plastic against the winter weather.

There's a lot to do to prep for winter even on my small estate. I raked enough leaves to save the lawn, I hope. My German grandparents and my mother loved trees, as do I. That has resulted my having twelve trees on my little corner lot. I think it's a German trait to like having lots trees nearby. When I traveled in Germany, I noticed most roads in the countryside were lined with trees. They had to have been planted that way because they were spaced evenly, the same distance apart and same distance from the road. My mother planted a maple and a crab apple tree. They are now huge things. Beautiful. I planted two myself – a lilac tree and a maple. They are now over 20 feet tall. I keep eyeing beautiful trees in Litchfield and wish I could plant a few more, but I must accept that I have enough.

I have noticed that the older trees lose their leaves before the younger. That makes sense I guess. Older people lose eyesight, hair, balance, and teeth before younger people. There are exceptions, I know, but that does seem to be the rule.

Researchers say that trees communicate with each other. According to forester Peter Wohlleben, a German of course, trees help each other. In Africa, when giraffes nibble on acacia leaves, that tree emits a gas warning other acacias to pump tannin into their leaves – a chemical that can sicken and even kill any animal that tries to eat them. I am going to have to read his book, *The Hidden Life of Trees*.

I wonder what my trees are talking about behind my back or rather over my head.

Yum!

Holidays mean family gatherings, parties, churchgoing, and food, lots of food, goodies of all sorts.

That got me thinking about the food I have loved over the years and the memories surrounding those good eats. My love of food began very early, as follows:

"'Cream cone, I'm going to Acky Town to get a 'cream cone."

That's what I told the farm wife who took me into her kitchen. I was three years old and had walked from my farm through the corn fields. I was on my way to Acton, a little town where my mother bought groceries. And where she bought me ice cream cones.

The lady had seen me trudging by her house and knew a 3 year old should probably not be out on her own. She invited me in, gave me a cookie, and called my mother who – much relieved -- came to get me. She drove us both to Acton where we got some 'cream cones.'

Ice cream cones figured in a dramatic event in my life which I was too little to remember but the rest of my family definitely did. My older brother Calvin and I were sitting in the back seat of our car eating ice cream cones. (Again with the cones!) I finished mine before he did. So, naturally, I figured he should give me his. He said, "No.!" I insisted – he resisted -- calmly and slowly licking his ice cream cone.

Enraged at being thwarted, I flew into a loud, angry tantrum. I screamed and kicked and bawled my head off. I was in the wrong but that did not matter. I wanted what I wanted. My father, who usually pampered me, finally was soon fed up. He stopped the car by a school house with a pump next to it. He grabbed me and pumped cold water on my head until I shut up. Shocking to me but it did not stop me loving ice cream.

Ice cream was the goal for me again when my parents drove to Manannah from another farm we lived on. For adults, Saturday was for shopping and socializing. I stood up in the back of the car behind my mother, my sweaty hand clutching the nickel I was given to buy – you guessed it -- an ice cream cone.

As my parents bought groceries and met friends, I sat in front of a building on which a movie was projected. Along with lots of other little kids, I sat watching the movie, my ice cream melting down my arm, enthralled by the movie stars I saw on the side of the building.

Then, another favorite: pop. Grape pop. What a treat. There is a photograph of me, my brother and two cousins, ranging in age from nine to four, seated on a bench beside a lake, drinking our pop. I also liked cream soda pop. No Coca Cola or Pepsi or diet anything for us. I remember fishing around in a large ice-filled metal tank to find my bottles of pop. In the summer, those tanks sat next to gas stations and lakeside concession stands.

Malted milks. Yum. We bought them at the popular Litchfield diner, Janousek's, for fifty cents. When we lived in town, my mother and I often went to movies and as we walked home and came near Janousek's, she would sometimes say, "Want a malted milk?"

Did I want a malted milk? I guess so. Wow. They were thick, filled with a mixture of vanilla ice cream, chocolate syrup, and malt. The waiter would fill a large glass with the malt and set that in front of me along with the still half full metal container the drink was mixed in. I remember watching beads of water condense on the outside of the silver container and trickle down to the table. That was one big malted milk.

For a time, you could still get one of those sublime malts at the Parkview restaurant which sits where Janousek's used to be. It cost a little more than fifty cents but it was so delicious; just like the old days.

For several years, we lived on the south shore of Lake Ripley, just outside Litchfield. We often fished off our dock. The bullheads were good to eat but hard to clean. You needed a pliers to do it. The meat was succulent and flavorful. There was so little time between catching and frying the fish that its muscles would contract in the pan making it look as though they were still alive. They weren't but it made a lively display for the waiting diners. Sunfish did not jump in the pan but were much sought after. My mother said the smaller sunfish were tastier than the big ones. I liked them at any size. A delicate taste.

A side note about sunfish: they will nibble on your skin if you stand still. My brother was swimming with us in Lake Minnie Belle when a big sunfish acted as if it had a crush on him. It followed him as he moved away to avoid being nibbled. But the fish circled him for several minutes like a persistent puppy until It finally got tired of the game and swam off. Bullheads nibbled at our legs too. It didn't hurt but made us jump around a bit.

My mother was a good cook. She said she learned how from my father's mother. Her own mother, our sweet little grandmother, was not a good cook. She made edible, nourishing meals but they just weren't that tasty. Though I will say she grew some superb raspberries that burst on your tongue with a sharp, sweet flavor. My mother baked cinnamon rolls and bread and chocolate cake, all from scratch of course. No mixes in those days. She worked full time in a factory but on those days when she was sent home early, I'd get off the school bus overjoyed to smell baking bread or cinnamon rolls.

Her chicken soup with dumplings was heavenly. She made the dumplings out of cream puff dough, rich in butter and flour and eggs. It was a tricky recipe. I grew up to try my hand at it and failed at least half the time. You melt butter and flour in a medium hot pan, stirring carefully until it just cooks enough to coat the bottom of the pan. You let the dough cool a bit and then you quickly dump in eggs and stir like a crazed person until the whole thing forms a lump. With a spoon you take bits of that lump and gently lay them into slightly simmering chicken soup. When the bits of dough rise to the top, they are done and you have the lightest, creamiest, softest little dumplings you have ever tasted. You could also make cream puffs from this recipe. My father's sisters – Gertrude and Dagmar Stiff and Sina Linden -- had a half-serious competition to see who made the best cream puffs which they filled with either vanilla pudding or whipped cream. Both were delicious. As to the competition, I agreed with whoever was serving me at the moment

Now, for the big finish, the yummiest dish of all: Fresh oyster stew. I first tasted it as a child. It was a treat only my father and I enjoyed. He'd bring home a pint of fresh oysters, and while I waited at the kitchen table, he heated them up in a pan with milk, butter, and salt and pepper. Timing was all; too hot and the oysters would be tough; not cooked long enough and they would not taste right. Daddy knew just how to do it. He'd fill two big bowls, crumble some saltines into them, and we'd dig in. Heavenly. A special treat because oysters were only available in Litchfield during the winter holidays. To this day, I make oyster stew every time I can get them. It is one of the best legacies my father left me and sweet memories of him and me enjoying our own little feast. Yum.

OF MICE AND ME

I have watched those scenes in movies where the heroine jumps on a chair and shrieks, "Eeek, a mouse!"

I never understood that. I have no fear of mice. In fact, I find them cute and sometimes funny.

In my New York apartment I had a mouse buddy. I was especially lonely after my husband died, so when I saw this little brown mouse moseying across the kitchen floor, I said, "Hello. How's it going?"

Yes, he was moseying. I could see the kitchen from the bedroom. He was no more than five feet away and headed for the dressing room.

I said, "Hey, there's nothing to eat in there."

He didn't even flinch but kept right on going. Just seconds later, he came back out.

"See," I said, " I told you there was no food in there."

But then, I recovered my human senses and clapped my hands loudly. He raced into my tiny bathroom. "There's nothing in there either," I shouted after him.

Where could he possibly hide in there? I got up

and searched the room. All it had was a tub and a sink in it. No mouse holes that I could see. Nothing. He had just vanished.

Another time, I was once again lounging in bed reading. I saw a movement out of the corner of my eye. I looked. There he sat. Just looking at me.

"Well, how are you? What do you want?"

He blinked, turned and walked, more like sauntered, into the dressing room.

"What do you like in there? I don't get the attraction," I yelled after him.

Common sense set in and I decided I would try to trap him. Not anxious to see what would happen but I knew it was what I should be doing. People were telling me they "chew through things" and can cause all kinds of trouble.

Not to mention leaving behind their tiny rice shaped poops. I got out one of my mouse traps. It hadn't been used for years. It had a strong spring on it which I always trapped my fingers in. After several snaps on my fingers and a lot of swearing, I finally got a tiny piece of cheese on the trigger of the trap. I put it down and went into the living room to read the paper.

The trap was five feet from me. It couldn't have been more than five minutes later that I got up to get more coffee. I looked down at the trap. The cheese had disappeared. Wait a minute, he'd have had to march out into the sunlit kitchen, and in full view of me sitting in the living room, just snatched the cheese and run. I had to admire his cheekiness.

I called my landlord and asked for help. He sent over an exterminator.

"Now for expertise," I thought.

I couldn't wait. He gave me a four by six piece of white cardboard with sticky material on a side.

"Put this where you think he'll walk. He'll get stuck and you can throw it out."

I suspected my mouse, by now I'd named him Mickey, was a bit too smart to do that.

But I said, "Okay, I will try it."

You know what happened. Nothing. That sticky thing caught my dust pan and my broom and me but my mouse had the sense not to touch it.

Before I left Manhattan permanently, I would spend half a year in Minnesota. I figured with me gone and absolutely no food of any kind in the place, Mickey would leave. Like a coward, I gave up my murderous plans for the little rodent and left him to his own fate.

That spring, I took off for Minnesota. Six months later, I returned. No mouse to be seen.

Great. I didn't have to kill the little bugger; he left of his own accord. Weeks later still and there was no sign of him. But then, one night as I lay in bed reading, I heard a scratching, rattling sound from the kitchen. My imagination. It's just the garbage shifting in the plastic bag in the can. Yeah. That's it. No, another rattly sound. Plastic crinkling. Damn. Mickey is back.

Shoot. I raced to the kitchen, opened the lid on the can and there, staring up at me was Mickey. "Well, welcome back, Mickey."

I grabbed the plastic bag, closed it tight, and sat it in the hall. It was way too late at night to go out to the big garbage cans in the back of the building. Next morning, of course, he was gone; he had chewed his way to freedom.

Years ago, we had no trouble with mice in New York. Lili, our cat, was fascinated by them, catching and eating them from time to time. At least, I assume she ate them.

One morning I found the bottom half of a mouse sitting in front of the sink. Lili wanted it but I snatched it away and flushed it. I worried she might get some disease from eating it.

Another time I noticed her sitting in the kitchen in a strange position. She was hunched over and shaking her head. Then, I noticed a mouse tail sticking out of her mouth. She opened it and out popped a very dizzy mouse. She stared at it, probably amused by its antics. I swooped down and slammed the heel of my hand on its head to knock it out. I picked it up by it tail and sent it down into the city sewer system. Lili was quite puzzled. I explained (yes, I talked to her all the time) "You can't eat that; it could have rabies or typhoid or whatever those things carry."

Lili wasn't satisfied and kept looking around for the disappearing mouse. Other than those incidents, Lili took care of the mouse population Sadly, Lili had died several years ago and the word spread among the mice -- no cat at Carole's place.

Without my cat, I had to fight the good fight alone. To do that, I resolved to take my garbage down to the cans daily. No temptation to mice. I gave up on traps and sticky cardboard. With no food easily available and me stomping and clapping my hands, the mouse lay so low I almost never saw him.

Once in a while, I'd forget to empty the garbage can and I'd hear that telltale rustling in the plastic garbage bag. I didn't even bother to get up anymore. I knew that once I left the place for my annual six months in Minnesota, I would come back to a mouse-free apartment. Mouse-free for a few months at least until the word got out. Carole's back with goodies.

I talked about Mickey so much that my mother brought him to life for herself. She imagined him with a cane and a top hat living with his little family in the bottom of my garbage can.

"When you're gone, they all go back to Ireland," she said. Why Ireland?

"Oh, he seems Irish to me. That cocky way of his – not being scared and just sauntering across your kitchen floor, stealing cheese right from under your nose." I saw her point.

Lately, I am wondering if his relatives have immigrated to Minnesota. I live in a house, originally a log cabin, which records indicate might have been built about 130 years ago. Evidence and my own suspicions lead me to believe that I am sharing this little cottage with bees, bats, squirrels, and mice. I hear scratching sounds in the walls and ceilings from time to time. Lately, the mice have taken to a new hobby: they rattle silverware. I often have left dishes and silverware in the sink to be washed in the morning. Not any more. That changed after one night when I was reading in my bedroom when I heard a tinkling sound coming from the kitchen 30 feet away. What? Can't be.

Then again: tinkle, tinkle. It was the sound of silverware bumping against a glass bowl. I went to the kitchen and sure enough there was a dirty bowl with a spoon in it.

Of course the mouse was nowhere to be seen though he had left behind a tiny souvenir. I resolved to be much neater and wash dishes every night. No tinkling. Then, a new development: Again, at night, I heard the sound of an oven shelf being moved. I recognized that rattling sound. I knew the mouse was in the oven.

So, I turned on the oven and waited. In seconds out ran a very very panicked grey mouse. Ha. Gotcha. He raced along the kitchen floor and disappeared into the cupboard. I could find no hole but gone he was. That stopped mouse movement for quite a while. The word was out among the mice: Stay away or the giant will set you on fire.

One mouse did not get the message or was too hungry to be careful. Just the other night, I heard the silverware being moved around. I looked; I had forgotten to wash a bowl and a spoon. The hunt was on again.

I have to get serious about this. The scratching in the walls and ceilings doesn't bother me but the little buggers fooling with my silverware wakes me up. They are cute little things but this is just going too far for me to tolerate anymore. The war is on.

Update: Time has passed; I hired experts so I am now free of bats and bees and mice.

I AM NOT CHEAP, I AM LAZY

You might accuse me of being cheap when you learn what I do to avoid buying things. But, I am not cheap. I am lazy. I hate going into stores. I hate trying to decide which rug, bedspread, blouse, window shade, or well, anything at all to choose. I like what I've already got and try to make it last.

So, what I do is mend things, things that any sane person would replace at once. For example, one of my window shades developed a tear up one side; in time, that tear became three tears. I thought: darn, those tears let in the light. What to do? Buy a new shade? Of course not. That would mean getting into my car and driving to Menard's in Hutchinson, 36 miles round trip. Too much trouble.

Time passed. I put up with the torn shade for just so long and then – Eureka! I thought of a solution. Like Red Green, I love duct tape. I use it a lot for many purposes. I got out some white duct tape – to match the shade - and carefully, oh, so carefully, taped those tears shut. Perfect. Looks fine to me. To the really diligent homemaker I am sure it looks tacky and awful. But it works. The shade goes up and down and no longer lets in light.

I was mocked when a friend found out I had hired a seamstress to put patches on the worn out elbows and knees on a sports outfit I loved.

She said, "Why not buy a new outfit?"

Nope, it seems easier for me to extend the life of clothing I like. Of course, that meant finding material for the patches and driving 30 miles round trip to the seamstress's home, twice. No, this doesn't seem to make sense for a lazy person but it does for someone who hates to shop.

I mend my sweaters, nightgowns, and blouses. I don't have a sewing machine so my repairs are all handmade. And they look it -- if you're picky about stuff like that. I once posed for a professional photograph; I thought I needed an 8 by 10 for business. It's a nice picture but, much later, on looking closely, I noticed the clumsy hand stitching I had done to mend the sweater.

I had a caftan I finally had to give up as much too worn out to mend. But, not willing to throw it out, I tore it up and made dresser scarves out of it.

Without a sewing machine, I had to hand stitch the edges. No, actually, I hand stitched a couple edges but being lazy, I decided to leave some edges raw. I excused that as being an art statement. You buying this? I thought not. Just lazy.

I dropped my cordless phone and it broke into several pieces. Not wanting to shop (of course) I pulled out the duct tape and put it all back together. Looks kind of makeshift but it works fine. No need to buy a new one, unless you're a person who wants everything to be perfect. I mean, come on.

I am using an old keyboard as I type this. By now, you won't be surprised that I had some repairing to do. Some letters are worn off entirely or hard to read. My solution: I painted them with white fingernail polish.

Okay, now I know I've lost you. In fact, as I read that last paragraph, I've lost myself. That's ridiculous.

Okay, okay, my New Year's resolution will be: Buy a new dang keyboard. No, really, I might actually do it.

WHAT'S THAT ON MY CALENDAR? I CAN'T READ IT!!

My handwriting has been getting worse the older I get. I can read most of it but sometimes I can't. I have a note on my calendar for a particular date. It looks like two words. The second word is clear enough. "Bill" it says with an exclamation point after that. The first word is the puzzling part of the phrase. It could be "call" but it's too long a scrawl really to be that and I don't know a Bill I'd have call on a specific date. It could be "Cake" but why write "Cake Bill!"? I don't owe anyone for a cake. Or does it mean remember to cake Bill? Cake him with what and who is Bill?

Is it "Casket"? Casket Bill? My husband Bill passed away in 1998 – a bit late for a casket. He has had one for over two decades. Or is it "Cabin Bill"? No Bill I know has a cabin. Wait! On a closer look it could be "Read Bill!"

Am I referring to good old Bill Faulkner? Am I supposed to read a Faulkner novel for the Book Club? No, we plan to read *Persuasion* by Jane

Austen for our next meeting. There are other "Bill" writers I might make a note to read: Shakespeare, Baldwin, or Wordsworth for starters. No, unlikely I'd make a calendar note to read anyone for that matter.

    I guess I will just have to hold my breath and wait for what happens on or after the marked date to see what I missed. I wouldn't be quite so curious were it not for that somewhat ominous exclamation point after the phrase. If it is something to exclaim about, why can't I figure out what it means? Don't answer that.

MY LILAC TREE

Why is my lilac tree so temperamental? Last year, it would not bloom. This year there were 44 blossoms on it. That beats the record of two years ago when it presented 13 blooms.

The lilac tree is not like my lilac bush which blooms every year right on a schedule. The tree's flowers are white; the lilac bush's are, well, lilac colored. Purple. Both have lovely smells but different from each other. The tree's are more pungent and deeper than bush's.

I have consulted the experts about my tree not blossoming every year but have gotten no clear answers. Before you wonder about fertilizer and watering, never mind. I do that on a regular basis. Don't start backing away, but I think plants respond to their environment just as animals do. Just more slowly.

Could my lilac tree be moody? Some years it just isn't up to the work of bursting into bloom. I've had those times when I just took it easy for awhile. Why can't a tree? Peter Wohlleben, a German who studies trees, says they "have feelings and like to stand close to each other."

I planted a maple tree next to the lilac several years ago and their branches are almost touching. Could that be helpful to the lilac tree and account for its exuberant blooming this year? Could the maple getting closer make the lilac tree happy?

Later research has revealed that trees do not want to touch leaves; no matter how friendly they may be to each other. The competition for sunlight gets in the way. I guess those two trees will never hold hands or allow their leaves to touch. Shoot. Another romantic notion down the drain.

Meanwhile, I have praised the tree for this year's record-breaking outburst of flowers. Recently, researchers for the British Royal Horticultural Society found that talking to plants – including trees -- makes them grow faster. Especially if that voice is female. Hey, excuse me, I am quoting the Royal Horticultural Society. They ought to know. I think.

Of course, there will always be those who will say "pooh" to that. I say, give it a shot; it could work. But: It might be smart to do your tree-talking unobtrusively so no one can claim you've gone round the deep end. Even though being socially isolated for months because of the plague, you are probably already talking to trees.

FROM WILD TO TAME, A KITTEN'S TALE

Here begins the story of Kiki, whom I found one 20 below zero wintry day in February of 2024. At first I thought he was a female.

I named her Kiki. I decided a little grey kitten who showed up in my yard was a female. I found her after I heard a meow awhile ago and wondered where it was coming from. Then, I saw her racing from my yard across the street to hide in a garage. Neighbors said she was a stray.

Is this my destiny? Is she to be my kitten? I had lived with Lili, a calico cat, for 21 years. She was also a stray; we found her in the hallway of our apartment building. No one claimed her and she became a cherished pet. She was my friend, confidante, and playmate. When she died, Bill and I grieved for her for years; I still do. I have always wanted another cat but just could not commit. But now this: Is this little grey kitten meant for me? Is it fate?

But, she was terrified. She ate food I put outside for her but if I approached, she would back off and run away. And now, the taming began. Slowly, I am getting her used to me. I coaxed her into coming into my entryway to eat but I have to leave, return to the kitchen and shut the door between us. She ate and ran. Days later, she ate but stayed to examine the room.

She yawned and stretched but still ran if I opened the door between us.

More progress: the other day she not only sat in the entryway after eating, she also drank some water and wonder of wonders! Cautiously entered the kitchen after I slowly opened the door just a few inches. She sat and watched me as I sat across the room typing on my computer. When I turned to speak to her, she quickly left the room. After watching me from the entry way for a few moments, she disappeared like a ghost.

Is she feral? The jury is still out and may be for weeks. Whether feral or socialized, I will take her to the Hawk Ridge Animal Shelter in Willmar. They will check her health and vaccinate her as needed. If I want to adopt her, I can, for a modest fee, but only after they have checked me out to be sure I can give her a good home. If she is feral, however, my research suggests she would not be a good or happy indoor house pet.

If she continues to be more and more brave, it is possible that Kiki may be my next Lili. If she is a female, that is. That remains to be seen. Kiki may have to renamed. Or not. Are male cats offended if given female names? T.S. Eliot, the great poet, and cat lover, claimed that all felines have their own private secret names only they know. And never reveal.

So, whatever we call them probably doesn't matter a bit to them. They respond to whatever name we give them because they love food and being petted. Don't we all?

FROM WILD TO TAME – UP DATE

The stray kitten, Kiki, made some progress today. She not only entered my kitchen, keeping a wary eye on me, but she also ventured into the living room.

I sat very still at my computer as she poked under the dresser and the coffee table. Something startled her; she suddenly raced past me to the entryway where she stopped and turned around to watch me through the half open door.

I got up and went into the bedroom to change into my outdoor clothes. When I came back, Kiki zoomed out of the porch, a grey blur, and slid in a wide circle on her way back to the entryway where she stopped to keep an eye on me.

Okay, I thought, she's more confident now. She has examined my entryway, kitchen, living room, and porch.

Next: can she play? Or has she become so fearful she just can't. To tempt her back into the kitchen, I put down a bowl with a small amount of cream in it. That got her: She inched her way back into the kitchen and lapped up the milk. When she was done with that, she took up her watch-cat pose to observe me. I wrinkled up a small piece of paper and tossed it. Surprise, surprise. That frightened stray kitten forgot her fears and moved up on that ball of paper and batted it across the floor and then batted it again. For the big finish she tossed that crumpled piece of paper high up into the air. I almost cried. A playful kitten still lives in her!

But, I had errands to run. So Kiki and I had to part ways. She watched me as I stood up and came slowly near her as I moved toward the open door. She reacted quickly and raced outside as fast as she could.

While at the store, I bought a yarn ball for her. It had a bell inside it that tinkles when it's moved. I bet Kiki will get a kick out of it. She did; more on that later.

I hated putting her outside at night. But, she needed to learn how to use a litter box. I bought one and waited for her to get the idea. Wow. She looked it over and about an hour later, she figured it out and used it. Eureka! She was now an indoor cat. No need to go out into the cold fearsome night.

Kiki sneezed several times one day so before she knew what was happening I swooshed her into a carrying case and dashed off to see our local veterinarian.

Kiki furiously protested this intrusion, but the gentle doctor and his assistant knew their business and got the job done.

BIG NEWS: Kiki is a male! And healthy -- except for bronchitis for which he was given a shot of antibiotic. The Vet said he's about 8 months old and weighs 8 pounds. Kittens, I read, do not become adult cats until they are one year old.

On Kiki's next visit he will be given more shots and other ministrations to improve his lot in life. But that can wait. He may not be so traumatized next time as he becomes more socialized. Or not. We shall see.

I think Kiki is a gifted kitten. I know, everyone thinks THEIR pet is smart. But get this: One day, I said, "Go find those yarn balls you lost."

I then went into the bedroom to read. About half an hour later, I came out into the kitchen. There, in the middle of the room on a scatter rug, sat three yarn balls.

They were equidistant from each other forming the 3 points of a triangle. I say no more.

Kiki the cat, when he realized his IQ was 184, like Truman Capote.

FROM WILD TO TAME – SETTLING IN

He watches the night, Kiki does.

A few short weeks ago, Kiki, the former stray, recoiled from human contact. Today, he is attentive to his new home and roommate to the point of excess. Where once he flinched if I looked at him, he now crawls on me as I try to read -- pushing his nose against mine.

Today, he slept, dozed, and meditated for hours. A quiet time after a morning filled with playing, leaping, running, chasing a ball, a crumpled piece of newspaper, and gorging on his favorite food. After all that action, I resisted teasing or otherwise interfering with his contemplative mood.

At 9 PM he wandered into the kitchen. He crunched a few dry food tidbits. He disappeared -- I thought. But there he was in his usual spot -- watching birds. But it was dark now. Settled comfortably on a folded blanket on the day bed, he kept his vigil. I had left the shade up near him so he could see the outside world at night.

The sight mesmerized him. After all, it was his

former home. He could run free then but he was threatened by the dark. No protection. No warmth. Dogs, people, cars – all frightening and dangerous. Now, he was safe, warm, fed, watered, and played with.

Yet, the freedom to come and go at will must still call to him. Is that why he stares so intently into the dark beyond the window? I saw nothing but he must have as he could not turn his head away. He saw things or imagined he did. That was his home once. Now, he is much better off. Does he thank his lucky stars? No, my guess is he accepts his fate, good or bad.

I can learn from this little animal: Patience, persistence, living in the moment. My guess is that Kiki does not think about whether he needs to lose a few pounds, or worry whether he's offended anyone. He is a totally genuine article.

But, I do think he may be an actor at heart. He definitely knows that the ball of yarn is not a mouse. I waved a feather toy at him and he leaped and jumped in delight. Then, he paused and looked into my eyes. I believe he KNEW it was me waving the fake "bird." Still, he went along with the gag and had a ball pretending he was chasing a real bird.

KIKI TAKES ARMS AGAINST HIS OWN PERSONAL SEA OF IMAGINED TROUBLES

It would appear that my highly energetic roommate, Kiki, the 9 month old former stray cat, has decided to do battle with various objects in my home.

These opponents include the threshold from my kitchen to my living room. How can that happen, you ask? There is a three inch rise to get from the kitchen floor to the living room floor. For some reason, Kiki took offense at this and has been clawing, biting, and wrestling with that rise almost from the first day he moved in. So far, he has not done damage to it but this is one persistent fellow so we shall see.

The kitchen scatter rug also offends him. He rolls himself up in it and then, like Cleopatra, unrolls himself with a flourish. He also grabs it in his fore paws and punches it with his back legs. What that rug has done to him I will never know, nor does he, I am sure. It too has apparently come through all this abuse intact.

I am also keeping a close watch on the window shades. He has bit and clawed them as he tries to get them out of the way so he can bird watch. I shout NO and raise the shade out of harm's way. I THINK he gets the idea. Months later, he has found a graceful way to get behind the shades without tearing them. Smooth move.

He does battle with some objects I cannot see. Either his eyesight is better than mine, (quite possible), or he has a great imagination (almost certainly). Sometimes, he pauses in his warfare and gazes into my eyes. It seems as if he can't quite focus. Does he need glasses? Or is it that he can't figure out what kind of animal I am.

I wonder about that myself, by the way. On the other hand, I am pretty sure Kiki knows very well what kind of animal HE is. And to be sure, we are both glad of it.

KIKI MEETS HIS OLD ROOMMATE

It was a peaceful evening about 11 PM. I was watching a movie on my DVD player; Kiki (my formerly feral cat) was on guard watching the night at his favorite windowsill nearby.

Suddenly, he leapt at the window screen, clawing at it ferociously. What? Were there bugs outside drawn to the light? Kiki did not listen to me as I tried to stop him scratching at the screen. Then, it hit me.

I ran around to the front door and turned on the deck light. And there was the reason for the uproar. Kiki's old roommate and pal from across the street was standing on the deck railing facing Kiki on the other side of the screen. I recognized the cat from another time when Kiki slipped outdoors for a rendezvous.

I shouted, "You go home. Go home."

He immediately leaped down and disappeared into the night. I came back to see Kiki jump off the windowsill and race about the house greatly excited. Took a few minutes for him to calm down.

Fortunately, my newly installed pet screens suffered no damage from the two cats' encounter. I felt sad that Kiki – an indoor cat -- was a prisoner in my home. Still I was reassured by remembering he had escaped four times before and always came back home of his own accord. He tasted freedom – once for six hours -- but chose to come back to me. He had made a decision. Yet, the urge to play with his pal was tempting.

If I let him out, it's likely he would come back but I do not dare do that for fear he might get lost, hurt, or killed.

Nobody gets to have it all, not even smart, beautiful Kiki.

THE BATTLE FOR CONTROL IS ON

My ten pound roommate wants to run my house. And I fear he's winning. A neutered, formerly feral, male cat, he goes by the name of "Kiki." He knows his name. Just say "Kiki" and he perks right up. Say "C'mere!" and he comes running.

He knows that I never call him unless it's for something good. Food, a squirrel on the deck, or birds eating birdseed outside the window, or a couple of dogs trotting by.

He loves to investigate everything. If he suddenly races by me tail down and low to the floor, I know someone is coming near the house. I have a watch cat you might say. He doesn't bark, he scoots away. Ding, ding, check it out ma'am. And it is always something, postman, friend, meter reader, or salesman.

He wants to control me. He wants to be fed NOW. Not on my schedule. He wants to be petted but for just so long and then he will pretend to bite and if you don't quit, it will become a real bite. You learn the rules fast. I have scars to prove it.

Cats are like that -- so say cat owners and veterinarians. I must be sensitive to their body language, we are told. A stiff body, switching tail, and you will cease and desist or else.

Controlling he may be, but Kiki likes to be reassured that he is okay. It's the middle of the night. I hear a quiet meowing from the living room.

I have learned to speak to him, I say, softly and I hope soothingly, "Kiki, everything's alright. You are safe and you are loved."

First time I did that I was surprised. He stopped meowing and it was quiet through the rest of the night.

Come to think of it, wouldn't it be lovely to have someone reassure you like that? Tell you when you are afraid that you are safe and loved? Maybe some people have that and I say good for you.

I think Kiki is extra smart. Or does every pet owner think that of their pet? Judge for yourself: I found Kiki standing on the toilet seat, the lid open and he, reaching down to the water. I said, "No, get off that. Don't stand on it when the lid's open." To my surprise, he leapt down and came over to me.

I said, "Watch this."

I got his attention. I went to the toilet nearby. I patted the closed lid.

"Jump on this. Then, get on the sink and play with the water."

With that I turned on the faucet just a bit so that a thin trickle of water came down, I repeated my instructions. I touched the toilet lid; I touched the sink and I played with the now streaming water.

"See? Wouldn't that be fun?" He came to sit by my computer. I said, "Think it over. I know you need to process this information."

About 30 seconds later, Kiki walked into the bath room, leapt onto the toilet lid, moved onto the sink and played with the water. Wait – What.? Did he understand sign language? Does he now speak English? Or, would he have done that anyway without my instructions? I think he understood my hand signals. He's done that before. He has sat in THAT chair when I so indicate. He has leapt up onto the table in the living room when I signal that he should do that. He has learned that when he does what I signal, it means something good will happen. He'll see action outside that window, he will enjoy treats, or will play with a new toy.

A few friends have gently suggested that I am maybe too involved with Kiki. They are right. I do need to back off -- even Kiki has indicated that. Sometimes he just jumps up and goes off to what I call his "office." It's a spot behind a rocker that is surrounded by other furniture. A little nook out of the way. I figure it's a refuge from his over-attentive roommate.

I respect that. We all need some 'me" time, don't we?

KIKI CULTURE

Kiki – my feline roommate -- and I have now lived together for a year -- ever since he showed me he knew what a litter box was for. He is an indoor cat and I am retired so you can imagine how much time we spend together in my very small home. As a result, we have developed a few rituals.

Occasionally friends drop by and I am happy to report that Kiki has become a social animal. Though he does run away for a few moments when guests first arrive, he quickly returns to check them out. He likes them all. He hops onto his chair by the table and watches and listens to our conversation. He enjoys being petted and talked to. After about five minutes, he leaves to pursue other interests. I think he has a short attention span.

Our close relationship has resulted in our sharing a kind of personal culture. One ritual that has evolved is the welcome home routine. If I leave the house for more than an hour, my return is greeted by Kiki bounding toward me, sometimes leaping into the air. I know what I must do: I take off my coat and immediately walk into the bedroom calling him to me. I sit on the bed; I gesture for him to sit beside me.

He does; I pet him and whisper sweet nothings In his ear. He purrs and looks up at me. I scratch his chin and cheeks and stroke his silky fur. After awhile, from three to ten minutes, his body stiffens and I know he is ready to go. A good stretch on the night table and he is off. We have never skipped this ritual. It's good for us both I think.

In the morning, I open the window in the entryway. The ice cold breeze comes in.

I say, "Come on, the window's open."

He races from wherever he is to leap onto the window sill . He smells the air and watches the yard and street. Anything that moves gets his attention. He sees some things invisible to me. He can stand the cold for about five minutes and then leaps down and I close the window. Brief as it is, it is a ritual we always observe.

He has recently added another routine. I spend a lot of time at my computer. He has become rather pushy about this. He comes up behind me, stands on his back legs and taps me on the back. I am supposed to pay attention. If I don't, he taps me again and again. Yes, it is food and/or play time. Who runs this place? You know the answer to that, don't you?

But, I shouldn't sit so long in one place anyway, right? So Kiki is doing me a favor by getting me up off my butt. That's my story and I'm sticking to it – I am NOT being bullied by a 13 pound housemate. So there.

KIKI AND THE AMERICAN PATRIARCHY

I recently watched a new-ish movie called MISBEHAVIOR, an unfortunate title for a very provocative film. It was a docu-drama about the birth of the Women's Liberation Movement in London. There had been growing protests across England but one demonstration made international headlines. Calling themselves the Womens' Liberation Movement, protestors shut down the 1970 Miss World pageant. The headliner was Bob Hope, who apparently never did figure out what was so bad about judging women by their looks and breast, waist, and hip measurements in a quest to name the most beautiful woman in the world. It was a very popular annual TV show.

With that demonstration the women's movement was born, ultimately resulting in a revolution in the way women were perceived. The David Frost Program also did a show on that subject in 1970. I was part of the staff and watched as Frost interviewed the emerging leaders of the movement, among them Gloria Steinem and Betty Friedan (author of the bestseller, The Feminine Mystique). They argued that women had been treated unfairly for too long, kept in second place by worldwide patriarchies. For example, they wanted equal pay for equal work, and they pushed for other changes that are now commonplace and – in some cases, fifty years later – still being fought for.

When the movie ended, I had to discuss this. It was too late to call anyone, so, (now here's the odd part), I went into the living room, leaned on the buffet and told Kiki, my cat, about it. He had been minding his own business napping in the big upholstered chair. I began, "Now, Kiki, being a cat, you may not be aware of what a patriarchy is. And being, a male, albeit neutered, even if you were aware you would not be effected by it."

Okay, sounds nuts, doesn't it? Lecturing my cat on the women's movement. But, the moment I started my rant, he had looked up and stared fixedly at me. I went on and on. I was on a roll. His gaze never wavered; he lay at ease but never took his eyes off my face. After a few moments, I began to feel uneasy. To have this intense gaze on me, especially from a usually easily distracted animal became unnerving. His English is minimal so I figured he must be entranced by my heightened energy and intensity. Maybe he wondered if there would be treats later. In the end, I ran out of gas and closed by thanking him for his attention and hoped he had a better understanding of the goals of the women's movement. I have to admit, though, that Kiki is an unapologetic narcissist so I am doubtful he did nothing more than wonder, "What the heck was THAT all about?"

PAUL NEWMAN

As a producer and writer for the shows I worked on, I spent time with many celebrities. I pre-interviewed guests, and then wrote up my notes and suggested questions for the host's information.

I was chosen to produce a 90 minute David Frost special on Paul Newman. That meant I needed to spend a lot of time with the star.

Newman seemed nervous when I met with him in his hotel suite. I noted he had bitten his nails to the quick. He restlessly scanned the room while we talked. We discussed what he would talk about, which movie clips to use and what he would say about them.

He was polite and courteous. Although he was attentive and pleasant, I sensed a melancholy air about him as if he were covering up a deep sadness. I was never to know for sure what might have caused it.

I read years later that he always felt guilty at leaving his wife and three children to marry actress Joanne Woodward. And, there was the untimely death of his son, an aspiring actor.

A brilliant artist and a good man, he donated

millions to charity through the profits of his company, Newman's Own, a popular brand of food products.

After taping the program with Frost, Newman invited me to go with Joanne Woodward and him to Elaine's, a popular restaurant. I agreed and joined them in their limo. I was charmed to note that as we drove to Elaine's, Newman tickled and teased Woodward making us all laugh at his antics.

SOPHIA LOREN

Sophia Loren was booked to be interviewed on the David Frost Show and I was assigned to pre-interview her, get notes for David, and prepare her for the program.

She met me at the door to her hotel room. It was one of those swank East Side hotels where movie companies placed their big stars. She was publicizing a new movie.

The big news for her was that she had had two sons after months and months spent in bed during the pregnancies. She had tried for years to become pregnant but it wasn't until a new gynecologist devised a plan which resulted in success.

The other big news was that her husband Carlo Ponti had given her a huge diamond ring which she was happily showing off. Sadly, she flashed the ring on the Frost Show and was promptly robbed of it. Thieves broke into her hotel room. It doesn't pay to advertise sometimes.

At our meeting, she was as glamorous, graceful, and gorgeous as expected. But what was not expected was her friendliness and sense of humor. An Italian woman with her who seemed to be a very close friend. They were both quite gracious. I asked my dutiful questions and discovered that she would talk about anything.

After some social niceties, I rose to leave the luxuriously decorated living room of her suite. The two women escorted me to the door and we stood there a moment. I turned to Ms. Loren and for some reason decided to be quite silly.

I said, "Miss Loren, I have asked you many rather personal questions about your private life." She nodded and smiled. "It seems only fair," I went on, "that you should now have that same opportunity: Is there anything about MY private life you would like to know?"

The two women stared at me for about two seconds and then we all three burst out laughing. Sophia, her friend, and I instantly understood the ridiculousness of the whole situation and found it funny.

We all three knew that no one gave a rat's behind about my private life, or indeed, Loren's friend's private life. This was the drill: you become famous; people want to know what makes you tick. If you are not famous, no one cares what make you tick except, maybe, someone who loves you.

I have had a special fondness for Loren since that day.

LEE MARVIN

I was nervous as I prepared to pre-interview Lee Marvin for his appearance on the David Frost Show. Most actors are big on charm; they have to be to be successful.

But Marvin had a different reputation. A rough, tough character actor for years who had recently broken through to leading man roles. He was a big star. How would he treat me?

When I arrived at his hotel suite, he was in a meeting with several men who left then. He asked me to join him on a settee.

Smiling and pleasant, he asked, "Would you like a cup of coffee?"

"Yes, thanks," I said.

With that, He jumped up, grabbed a used cup, went to the sink nearby, washed and dried it carefully, filled it, and presented it to me with a flourish. Wow, I thought, Lee Marvin washing dishes for me. What a job I have! And, he was courtesy itself.

He sat back down on the settee and turned to me with a smile. I asked the usual questions: What do you want to talk about on the show? I asked a few questions of my own: reminding him of his war injury for one thing -- he was shot in the buttocks during World War Two. He laughed about that story.

He was attentive and listened closely. I took my notes, took my leave and put him on my list of real humdingers. Smart, funny, talented, and good looking. You never can assume.

DEADLY BLACKBIRD BATTLE IN MY BACKYARD

This morning I opened my door and found a blackbird lying upside down on my deck. It was dead. No obvious injuries but when I held it, I saw its neck was broken.

Earlier that same morning, I'd seen half a dozen blackbirds chasing one another near my pie tin with the birdseed in it. Two of them appeared to be seriously squabbling.

When I walked into the yard after checking out the dead bird, I saw that the pie tin had been knocked onto the grass. That was unusual. It had clearly been quite a battle scene. I'd seen birds chasing one another. but why this time, a killing?

To my surprise, my research revealed that occasionally blackbirds will fight to the death. If their territorial birdsong doesn't scare away competitors, the defending bird will go in for the kill.

But why had the defeated bird chosen to die in front of my door? Was he fighting for his life on my deck? Had he tried to escape his killer but could only make that far? A mystery.

The poet Alfred Lord Tennyson once described nature as "red in tooth and claw." And, the other day in my backyard, the black bird murder proved that to be true.

COUNTRY SCHOOL RULES AND GAMES WE PLAYED

Ever wonder why our grade school teachers wanted us to tell them whether we needed to go number one or two when we held up our hands to go to the toilet? Do they do that anymore? What in the world did they need to know that for? What business was it of theirs whether we had o urinate or have a bowel movement? I call that a serious invasion of privacy.

Comic Rodney Dangerfield had a joke about that: "I was robbed the other night. Guy had a gun. I got so scared, I went number three."

I remember my student days in the one-room school house I attended from grades one to three. It was on highway 16 north of Grove City. Was there a kindergarten? I don't think so.

Grades one through eight were all in the same room. We learned together. I used to watch the second and third graders when I was in first to see if I could learn what they did. The teacher finally gave up and moved me into second grade before it was time. Easier for her that way, I guess.

During recess we played games. I remember "anny anny over", probably a corruption of some actual words. We'd divide up into two teams, one on each side of the school house. One team would shout "anny anny over" and throw the ball over the roof.

Then, the other team would try to catch it and run around the building to tag the kids who threw the ball. Whoever ended up with all the kids on one side won.

Then, there was "pum pum pull away", two teams lined up facing each other. Someone was elected to be the "guardian" in what was called "no man's land" between the teams. The guard would shout "pum pum pull away" and all the kids would race toward each other to line up on the opposite sides. The guardian would try to tap as many kids as he could three times on the back. These kids would also become guards and the drill would start over. The game ended when all the kids were tapped and there were none left on either team.

Oh, and don't forget "Statue" and "Captain, May I?" In "Statue" a leader would twirl another player around and let go. The player would have to hold whatever position he ended up in. The object of that game escapes me now.

"Captain, May I?" had a duly-designated "Captain" in charge who stood on the goal line. The others would have to ask permission to move. If you forgot to ask permission, you went back to where you started. The object was to reach the goal line before anyone else. Then, you got to be Captain.

I liked Red Rover, Red Rover. Again, the kids would split up into two teams, line up holding hands and face each other. One team member selects someone on the other team and calls out: "Red Rover, Red Rover, send (whoever) over." The chosen team member races toward the other team and tries to break through the line. If she succeeds, she brings one of that team back to join her team. If not, she becomes part of the opposing team. The game ends when everyone's on one side.

I remember kids playing King of the Hill. Pretty simple. One person stood on a rise in the yard. "I'm King of the Hill," he would say. All the other kids were supposed to see if they could push him off and whoever did would become king. Pretty simple. I do not remember girls playing that game. The teacher did not like that game as it often lead to fights.

I don't remember bullying among the kids. Certainly, there could have been with ages in the school house ranging from six to 14. I have no bad memories of my days in the one room school house in the country. My brother and I walked to that school, trudging along about two miles through all kinds of weather.

My mother said if the snow and winter winds were too heavy, she would give us a ride. But that wasn't often; my brother doesn't remember ever getting a ride. One of the best memories I have of those long walks to school was listening to the meadowlarks singing as they swayed above us on the electric wires overhead. I don't remember being cold but we must have been. I can still hear the squeak of the frozen snow under our feet; the crunch of the gravel on the road, and the dusty dry rustle of corn stalks in the fields and dead weeds alongside the road. Some kids rode horses to school. We had horses but they were work horses and could not be spared to carry us to school. Amazing really, there'd be a great outcry today if children were expected to walk so far to school. I don't think that hurt us -- maybe it gave us good old fashioned grit.

I LIKE DIRECTING TRAFFIC

I get a kick out of telling drivers where to go. I was a professional at it; I worked in a large parking lot where people left their cars and took a bus to the State Fair. My brother hired me; he was the foreman of a big lot in St. Paul. He'd been doing it for years.

It was fun but serious, hard work where you were running around all day. At the end of the first day, I couldn't feel my legs from the knees down. I made about 400 dollars at the end for several days on the job.

I could never do that work today; but every so often I like to practice my hard-won skill.

First day at the parking lot, I realized I had to be a total dictator. Second, I must establish eye contact with the drivers. Then, using precise hand signals, I told them when to move, where to move, when to turn, how far to go and when to STOP. It's amazing how obedient people can be to totally firm, no-questions-asked directions given by a serious, unsmiling traffic controller. Of course, I always thanked them for following directions so well. They were happy to be praised.

Every now and then since that job several years ago, I get the urge to practice controlling other drivers. For example, when it's unclear at an intersection who should go first, I instruct the other driver to go ahead, using a firm, clear hand signal – precise, minimal. It works immediately.

Or, I tell them to pass me by when I've had to pull over for some reason. I roll down my window and signal with my arm that they should go around me, NOW. And they do immediately. They know I am not drunk, insane, or a fool. I know what I'm doing and won't pull out in front of them. At least, I hope that's what they think.

I am often surprised at how little motion it takes. Drivers are very observant once we've made eye contact. That works with pedestrians too. I often slow and allow them to cross the street even if I am not at a stop sign. Unless, of course, I'd be holding up traffic to do so, then the pedestrian has to wait in the usual way.

Only one driver just would not obey me. We met at the same time at a four-way intersection. Our eyes met and I signaled him to go ahead. But, no, he signaled that I should go ahead. I did with a wave of thanks. He apparently did not know that in such circumstances, it is the car on the right that has the right of way. He was on my right. I never argue; it's safer that way. Besides, he had a chance to be courteous; we really can't fault that, can we?

MY SISTER MYRNA DIED OF COVID

Oh, what a loss was there. Her quick smile; her humor, her surprising wit.

Her little bald head weaving back and forth above the wicker basket on the farmhouse kitchen counter. That's how I first saw her. I was three and a half years old, just barely tall enough to see over the counter. I remember how sweet she smelled with baby powder sprinkled all over her.

My sister, Myrna.

When she was older and could walk with me, we would stroll arm and arm singing songs we made up. In the spring we'd wander the farm and once walked into a muddy field. Myrna's feet became stuck; I couldn't to get her out.

I ran for mother shouting, "Myrna's stuck in the mud!"

Mother pulled her out. We never found her little boots.

We liked to dip our feet in the cows' water tank in the barnyard. Mother disapproved but thought it was so cute she took a picture of us posed over the tank in the act of lowering our feet into the water.

I always felt I was her guardian. Many pictures of us as children has me watching her as she gazed happily and eagerly into the camera. I always held her hand when we had to cross a street.

One day she said, "I'm too old for that."

We never again held hands crossing the street. She was right to declare her independence from her older sister. Something she had to remind me of many times when I tried to advise her more than she wanted me to.

Her quick wit was astonishing. She often made people burst into laughter at her often outrageous but funny remarks. Her reputation for telling jokes became well known; so much so she was asked to perform at a retirement party at the Veterans of Foreign Wars Club. She enjoyed it so much she hated to stop.

Her reaction to her own performance: "They laughed their asses off."

Much later in life, she knew her faculties had begun to fail when she realized her joke telling days were over. "My timing is off and I can't remember the punch lines," she said sadly one day. But till the last, she could still come up with impromptu witticisms on the spot. For example, I asked her once if she said grace before a meal.

She said, "Only if I'm afraid of the food."

Myrna's life was shadowed by mental illness. She had been married only a year when at 19 she suffered a psychotic break. She was diagnosed with schizophrenia and institutionalized for a month. With the help of a psychiatrist, electric shock therapy, and anti-psychotic drugs she was able to return to her life.

But schizophrenia is a chronic disease and from time to time Myrna needed to be hospitalized. Fortunately, for at least the last forty years of her life, she did not need hospitalization, a fact she was proud of. She always took her drugs. Myrna did not want anyone to know about her struggle with schizophrenia and outside her family very few did. Dealing with life's stresses was very hard for her. Sometimes she feared a breakdown when she faced especially difficult times. When she was diagnosed with breast cancer, when her father, then her mother and then her husband died, she was afraid of losing her sanity. But she didn't; she came through despite her fears.

I was so proud of her. I remember sitting on the curb waiting for the Litchfield Watercade parade to start. Then, we'd hear the boom, boom of the Litchfield Drum and Bugle Corps; the parade had begun.

We couldn't see them right away but then suddenly, there she'd be: Myrna in her white drum majorette costume high stepping along, whirling her baton and throwing it high up into the air. She was the head of the parade, leading the Corps as they marched behind her. They were excellent musicians and she was an excellent baton twirler. She'd throw her baton higher than the buildings on Main Street, twirl around and around and then catch it behind her back. She was magical.

And, she was beautiful. She was chosen to be a candidate for queen of the Litchfield Watercade and later, asked to be a candidate for queen of the Hutchinson Water Festival. She loved it and was flattered to be selected. She wasn't vain and enjoyed the fun of it.

I always envied her daring. We lived by Lake Ripley and we were in the water all the time in summer. I never dared dive off the Lake Ripley dive tower but Myrna did. She was determined to perfect her dives. With a T-shirt over her bathing suit to protect against the pain of belly flops, she practiced jack knives, swan dives and other difficult dives over and over until she was satisfied. She was recognized for her skill and one year was asked to perform for a program presented as part of the Litchfield Watercade.

Rollerskating was popular when we were teenagers. Myrna was so good at it that she was asked to join a troupe of professional skaters. They called themselves "the Westerners" and toured the Midwest as "the world's only square dance roller skaters." The highlight of their career was a performance at the Grand Ol'Opry in Nashville alongside headliners Johnny Cash, Ferlin Husky and Minnie Pearl.

Myrna married her childhood sweetheart Marvin Maher in 1957. After a few years in Minneapolis, the two returned to their hometown. Marvin established a home construction business and Myrna assisted him.

They traveled, socialized with friends, and spent time with their families.

Marvin died of leukemia in 2010 and not long after that Myrna moved into an assisted living apartment. Her needs increased and she moved to the Lakeside nursing home in Dassel. She enjoyed a pleasant life there until Covid 19 found her before there were vaccines. She died after a three week illness.

She was 82.

HOLDS ON HAPPINESS

I was reading a Jane Austen novel when I came across a passage in which one of the characters talks about holds on happiness. She is telling a friend about another friend who has discovered a passionate interest in daffodils. That is so wonderful, she says, now she has another hold on happiness.

A "hold on happiness." The idea started me thinking about what my "holds" were. I remembered the day I told my brother, Calvin Peterson, about one of them.

We were driving around Minneapolis doing errands and decided to stop for a snack.

I saw a bagel store and asked him if he'd ever had a bagel. "Yes," he said, "once."

"What was it like?" I asked.

"It had blueberries in it."

"Oh, oh. That's not a bagel," I told him. "I'm from New York City and I know what a bagel is supposed to be like. Come with me. I'll order an authentic bagel at this place."

I told the waiter to slice a plain bagel in half, toast it, smear it with cream cheese, add a slice of tomato, and a slice of onion, and then top it off with a slice of smoked salmon. Slam it all together; cut it in half and hand it over. He did.

"Now," I said, "that is a bagel the way it's supposed to be served. See what you think."

We silently chewed our way through the thing. When we finished, I asked, "So, what do you think?"

"That is really, really good. I like it."

"Well, now, you have another hold on happiness. Next time you're feeling blue, order that. It's dependable."

My other holds on happiness seem to be very simple, and cheap, too. I get a mellow feeling of happiness just slicing through the water when I take a swim at the local motel pool. And I really get a kick out of floating in Lake Manuella staring up at fleecy white clouds drifting across a bright blue sky.

Then there's the mornings: I love to lie on my daybed, a cup of good coffee in hand, and watch the world pass by my porch windows. The caffeine lifts my spirits and the birds, squirrels and humans going about their business keep me in a gentle state of bliss. Plus, now, I have a silky furred cat who lies beside in the sunshine.

I also get a good feeling when the lights go down at the movie house. I hunker down in my seat and smile as I wait for the film to start. An adventure is about to begin.

I like watching my sister, Myrna Maher, tell jokes. She gets a twinkle in her eyes and her whole body seems to rise up in anticipation as she captures the audience and leads them through her story. Then, the punchline; the listeners erupt into laughter. She smiles and her eyes half close in the pleasure she feels in making us laugh. I laugh at the joke but more than that, it makes me happy to see her so happy. Once again, she has woven a spell, taken us on an imaginary trip, and then, made us all laugh with her.

It's a pleasure watching people do what they're good at. I had my roof shingled a couple of years ago. I hired Don Holmgren, a man reputed to be very good at that. It turned out he was. Even though I knew nothing about the roofing process, I could tell he was a professional. He worked efficiently, every night cleaning up debris left over from the day's work. He was confident without being arrogant. When he met my nephew, an expert in construction, who came by to take a look, he was unperturbed and welcomed him as a fellow professional. It was a pleasure to watch him move about the roof making steady and sure progress. Though I'm sure he knew I didn't know anything about roofing, he regularly reported on his progress and what he planned to do next. He started on time and finished when he said he would. He was expertise in action.

For me, driving is another reliable hold on happiness. A sunny day in the country, Strauss waltzes on the CD player, a good car, and me, cruising the gravel roads, passing by cornfields and cows, scanning the sloughs for ducks, herons, muskrats, turtles, maybe even a couple pheasants and a deer or two.

Sometimes people ask me how I can enjoy Litchfield after living in "big, exciting" New York City. I, on the other hand, wonder how they can ask me that. Don't they know what they have here?

IN SEARCH OF A HERO

The statue stood alone in a small park next to a cemetery. He was a Medal of Honor winner from Anoka -- a World War II Marine who had thrown himself on a grenade to save his fellow soldiers. Every time I visited my brother, the late Calvin Peterson, at his home in Anoka, I passed the memorial. We both liked seeing it there in its lonely vigilance. But then one day, it was gone.

"I heard they moved it to another park," Calvin said, "No one knows where it is now."

"Let's find it" I said.

We always enjoyed driving around looking at "stuff" and interviewing passersby when we stopped along our way. But now, we had a mission: Finding Anoka's hometown hero's statue.

So on March 20, the first day of spring and my birthday, we began our quest.

We first stopped in a small park alongside the Mississippi. We called a park worker over to the car. He was an enthusiastic young man, busy cutting down buckthorn which he said was a nuisance. No, he knew nothing about our hero's missing statue. In fact, he'd never heard of it. He was delighted to chat, a vibrant fellow who loved his work. Not far from him, we talked to another man. He was older, a Centerpoint employee, in the middle of organizing his van. He knew nothing about our hero or a statue dedicated to him.

"Maybe they tore it down," he said. "You know how people can be these days."

"It's not a Civil War statue. It's a World War Two soldier. They aren't tearing those down," I said.

"Well, you never know," he said, "You know how people can be these days."

We agreed. You never do know.

As we moved along the city streets, Calvin caught sight of a beautiful white mansion on a hill. He wondered if we could investigate it and maybe find out more about our statue. It had parking spaces beside it so we figured it was open to the public. I parked out front and raced inside to find out what I could. Turned out the place had been built in 1857 and recently converted into a cozy restaurant called the Mad Hatter. We got lucky; the hostess knew all about our statue.

"Go north on 169," she said, "turn right on Main Street, left on 2nd Avenue, look to your left and there he is, alongside the Rum River."

We did and found him. But it wasn't the same. We had to park some distance from the statue and since walking that far was not possible, we examined our Marine with binoculars. There he stood, alone, holding his machine gun.

The lonely soldier was Marine Private First Class Eric Sorenson. He had been away from the States for only 18 days when he and his fellow Marines were caught in a battle in the Marshall Islands. They fought hard when suddenly a Japanese soldier threw a live grenade among them. Sorenson immediately threw himself on it. He said later he had been trained to cover the grenade. The lesson: "Don't let everybody get it just to save your own hide."

Most such acts of courage end in death but luck was on Sorenson's side. After numerous operations, he survived. He went on to serve in Korea and later was commissioned a Marine Corps officer. He died in Reno, Nevada, at the age of 80, leaving behind a large family and many friends. He also left behind a statue in an Anoka park, bearing mute testimony to his bravery that terrible day he leaped to save his fellow Marines.

Our mission accomplished, Calvin and I celebrated by going to a Dairy Queen near his home. We drove in, ordered two cones and asked the server how much we owed.

"Nothing," he said. "It's free today."
"Why today>"
"It's the first day of spring."
And, I told him, also my birthday.
It was a good day.

MY TEACHERS

I have had many teachers, from my mother to the common sense advice of friends, and colleagues, and others I have met over the years.

My mother taught me how to let go. At some point, as she busied herself with some necessary task, she'd stop and say, "That's good enough." Being able to stop like that has stood me in good stead when I needed to quit obsessing on how to make something better. That is a bottomless pit. Especially when it comes to creative work. It will never be perfect. Let it go. In television, if it isn't ready for air, it doesn't matter how much you polish it, it's over. You must declare it "good enough." She also used to say, "Never let housework get in the way of a good time." That's one of my golden rules, too.

About dieting: I once said to a slim friend, "I wish I were thin like you." A no-nonsense Scandinavian/American -- just said, "Don't eat so much." Good advice.

I interviewed Barbara Walters for a magazine article. I asked what she did when she felt overwhelmed with work. She said, "I cancel something." I've used that advice many, many times and it works.

Fellow Litchfield Writers Group member, Mike McNeil, one of the kindest people I've ever met, occasionally says to me, quietly , "Be nice, Carole." He knows me well enough to know when I am about to make a tart remark. I pay attention and find a gentler way to express myself.

My aunt Caroline Paysen told me to wipe down my shower walls. "Prevents mold," she'd say. I have been wiping down my shower walls for decades. I still get mold but only in the corners and then Clorox takes care of that.

My grandmother Gertrude Timm always swept away cobwebs; it was a rule of hers. "No good housekeeper allows cobwebs," she'd say. I now live in her home and you can bet there are no cobwebs around here.

When I was sixteen, My Uncle Harold told me to leave Litchfield and discover the world. "There's so much out there, Carole, go find it." I did and I'm still searching for and finding a lot of what's out there.

Photographer Richard Avedon told me he never ate until his work for the day was done. "Keeps me alert," he said. I do that; nothing but coffee until about 2pm. Not quite all day but I am so alert on caffeine people have to tell me to slow down so they can understand what I'm saying.

Mrs. Edna Whitaker, my Litchfield high school teacher, gave me advice that changed my life. I was a senior and one day in Study Hall, she came to my desk, leaned in closely, and said, with intense emphasis, "Carole, you MUST go to college. You MUST!" I had been planning to go to secretarial school but her words came at just the right time. I had saved some money and because of her advice I decided to use it to go to the University for one year – all I could afford. I managed to stick it out-- working my way through to a bachelor's degree and one year of graduate school at the University of Minnesota. Years later, I went on to a Master of Arts degree from New York University, and three years toward a Ph.D. Oh, if Mrs. Whitaker had only known what she unleashed that day in 1952! A perennial student. I may not be wise but I am educated.

But best of all, are the people who have made me laugh. They teach me to look on the funny side and there's always a funny side. My husband Bill, who we knew was terminally ill, even found the funny side of cancer. He'd say, "I'm eating for two, my tumor and me." Or: "why do I have to choose what pants I want to wear in my coffin? Who sees you below the waist?" Neil Shand, a comedy writer I once worked with on the David Frost Show said of a performance: "Everyone laughed so hard there wasn't a dry seat in the house." Friend Ron Markovich, who claimed to be an extra-terrestrial from the Planet Zorbo, told me about his assignments on Earth. He says he designed the Pyramids. "We'd have built more of them but we lost our funding." And then there are the writers who see the funny side: S.J. Perelman, David Sedaris, Dave Barry, Mark Twain, Peter De Vries, Stephen Leacock, Robert Benchley, and James Thurber. Joseph Heller, the author of "Catch 22", claims in his book "*No Laughing Matter*" that he was cured – through laughter -- of Guillain Barre syndrome, a debilitating disease that can kill. While he was trying to survive the disease, he watched funny movies, TV shows, and books, plus he enlisted funny friends, including Mel Brooks, to make him laugh. He finally did recover. He said laughter healed him. Moral of that story: keep laughing.

ACKNOWLEDGEMENTS

Many people over the years have urged me to write about my life and adventures. I would like to thank them here:

I am grateful to my mother who for years listened to me read my work to her and always said it was good, even when it wasn't. To further my embryonic ambitions, she bought me a typewriter and a desk when I was 13. No small thing; times were hard then.

My sister, Myrna, was a perfect critic. She did not know how to be false. If it was funny, she laughed, if it was boring, she would say so. If she was interested, she wanted to know more.

My brother, Calvin was always a steadfast fan. He insisted that I put my stories into a book – telling me over and over, "You are a good writer. People like reading your work. Publish!"

My father pitched in too. Proud of my ambitions, he gave me money to help with my expenses at college.

Others who have encouraged me include the late New York Times Media Critic Neil Postman, surgeon and bestselling author Dr. William Nolen, writers Joe and Nancy Paddock, TV producer/writer Andrew Smith, producers Peter Baker and Bob Carman, author Joan Oliver, Pia Lindstrom, Tom Brokaw, Jane Pauley, writers Phyllis and Gary Gates, Susan Drury, Karen Curry, Mary Loftness, Bill Covello, Neil Christenson, Jean Replinger, Brent Schacherer, writer Lawrence Milllman, Natalie Heiar, Tim Bergstrom, Mary Bacon, Carolyn Renfroe, Don Holmgren, Ron Markovich, Tom and Jennifer LaPlant, Ole Holst Petersen, the Red Hats Women's Club and the Litchfield Area Writers Group. Plus, people I do not know who have written to me or told me in person how much they like my work. And, of course, all those cat lovers who tell me they love reading about Kiki's adventures.

Thanks, thanks, thanks.

www.ingramcontent.com/pod-product-compliance
Lightning Source LLC
LaVergne TN
LVHW021236080526
838199LV00088B/4547